HOW TO BE A SUCCESS IN BUSINESS

Ida Greene

This Book Is Dedicated to the Millions of Small Business Women and Men, Who Want to Have a Successful Business But Lack the Skills to Get What They Want In Life.

Copyright © May 1, 2008 by P. S. I. Publishers, 2910 Baily Ave. San Diego, CA 92105. All rights reserved. No part of this publication may be reproduced or distributed, transmitted, transcribed, stored in a retrieval system, or translated into any language without the express prior agreement and written permission of the publisher.

ISBN 1-881165-14-0

**Attention Colleges and Universities, Corporations
and Professional Organizations**
Quantity discounts are available on bulk purchases of this book
for educational training purposes, fund-raising or gift giving.
For information contact:
**PSI Publishers, 2910 Baily Avenue, San Diego, CA 92105.
Tel. (619) 262-9951**

Contents

INTRODUCTION

A Journey Into The World of Business

The business world is the backbone of our great nation. It is a place where one can soar to great heights. It is also a place where you can drop to the depths of despair, so do what you can to make life easier and better for both yourself and your fellowman. Go often to the quiet resources of your inner self for there is where you will find the power, strength and determination to propel you forward when things go awry.

The world of high technology and the age of the computer are here. However, we will always need the resources of talented individuals, such as yourself, to bring ethics to a conglomerate giant—The Business World.

To succeed in the business world, you need to believe in yourself. To know that the world needs you and that you make a difference in the scheme of things. This may not always be apparent to you, for no one will ever say this to you. I am saying this to you now. I want you to know that you are needed in the business world. The world needs your input. You provide a piece of the puzzle that no other human being on the face of the earth can supply. You are unique. You are one of a kind among many.

The contribution you make may seem insignificant. But who among us can judge. Whatever talent you have to share be good at it. Know when to push and when to pull. Use wisdom and truth in all of your encounters with others. You have some influence others. But the person over whom you will have the greatest influence is yourself. Never allow yourself to become discouraged and disappointed. There is always tomorrow, and there will always be another sale. Spend time developing your talents, skills and inner resources. You are a product, are you a marketable product? Always seek to make yourself a better person and a better product.

As you along in the business world take the prayer of serenity with you—

**Lord, help me to change the things
I can change. To Accept the things
that I cannot change, and the
wisdom to know the difference.**

***

To get the most from *How To Be A Success In Business*
you will need a notebook. There are sections where you
will be asked to write down your answers or comments in
your notebook.

***

Chapter 1

How To Survive In The Business World

This book will help you focus on the key elements needed for success in any business. The first and foremost is you. You must develop yourself, then sharpen your skills, to withstand the volatile and sometimes hostile world of business. All businesses are a conglomerate of people with different personalities, who may at times seem to be speaking a different language.

A business is like an orchestra, each person plays a different instrument, but each has to be synchronized to produce a melody that is harmonious. The difference is that with an orchestra, you have a director to coordinate the loose factions. However, with a business, each person has to synchronize herself or himself with other business associates, and sometimes this can be disastrous.

Just as with a traffic jam, some people go, when they should slow down and look. Others go without checking all factors, and some are blinded by their ego and sense of importance.

The way to the top is much like a journey or a hunting trip. You may take many detours and it may seem at times that you have lost your way. However, the detour you take may turn out to be the missing information you need to complete your business journey.

So, pay attention to your intuition and hunches along the way, for they will seldom lead you astray. Our mind is always working to help us realize our dreams and desires. For instance, if you may say to yourself "I need to learn to be more subtle," your mind will find a way to accommodate you. The mind is always working to help us achieve our desires. You may think to yourself, "I wouldn't want to work for a strict boss". Your mind hears, "strict boss", and it begin to look for ways to give you your desire. A year later you may find yourself working under an autocratic executive in a large

1

corporation or you may become the strict boss. This new you was created through your self-image based on your needs. The key factor is to develop a healthy self-image to produce a positive self-esteem.

To have a healthy self-esteem, all people need the following:

- Security (acceptance by self/others)
- Self-Concept Identity, to belong
- Self-Worth, a feeling of importance to family, feel deserving, that you matter in life
- Desire/dream give you a sense of purpose, hopes, and ambition.
- Passion/Drive (enthusiasm-fire within, energy), thing/s you would do for no money.
- Support — mental, physical, and emotional. The self-esteem you spend months to develop can be destroyed in one minute, by a careless remark, or unkind word by someone. So tend to your self-esteem on a daily basis. It is the flower garden of your life.

If you are an aggressive, cutthroat type of person, you will need to learn subtlety. Because our mind works continually to accommodate us, it will provide an opportunity for you to learn how to be more subtle. Since learning a new skill is not easy, you may feel stressed. The road to the top of the business or corporate ladder is not always straight. You may have to detour along the way. However, the valuable skills you develop will provide a solid foundation from which to build, and act as a leverage to move you to the next rung of the ladder, as you move with patience. Patience is a trait you will need throughout your career; patience with yourself and others. Do not become wary and disappointed with yourself if you are not moving as swiftly as you had envisioned. For you could be gathering valuable information, that can assist you later in your climb up the business ladder.

As you move along your career path. Do a periodic assessment of your goals. Note where you want to go and what steps you need to take to reach your goals and objectives. Do this once a year, preferably at the beginning of the year. **Make this one of your New Year's resolutions.** Sit down; take out a 8 1/2 X 11 sheet of paper, turn it so the lines are vertical rather than horizontal; make 3 columns: Skills I possess, Skills I need to possess, and Skills necessary for me to possess. Be honest and truthful with yourself. If you feel you are too aggressive or passive, take an Assertiveness course, to have an objective database, from which to glean information.

If you have limited skills, either professionally or personally you will be replaced. Continue to look at ways you can improve your personal competence. See yourself as a piece of equipment. Are you an upgraded piece of equipment, or an outdated piece of equipment. Remember, a business needs value not a warm body. How valuable are you to the organization? Have you taken a course lately to stay abreast of the newer technology in your field? Can you be placed in more than one work environment within your organization?

How valuable you make yourself to an organization determines how far you go up the ladder. If you show the corporation or top management you can assist them in reaching their goals, a niche will be created for you.

You must know why you want to have a business, or be a businessperson before you embark on a career in business. The world of business is very different from that of being an employee. It is not for the feint of heart. You must be committed and determined to succeed in spite of obstacle or setback. The world of business is like a ship at sea; you may have smooth sailing one day, and be in the midst of a turbulent storm the next. You must have a good reason to be in business, and you will need to remind yourself often of your reason.

Besides having determination, persistence, and being a self-starter, you may need to work long hours. For you will have no one to complain to, or about if you are the boss (the buck stop with you). If your business is a success or a failure, it will be your fault.

You will not have anyone to blame or criticize except yourself. When you are in business for yourself, you may not get a yearly vacation. You go to sleep with the boss and wake up with the boss each day. And each day you determine whether you will wake up with a good or a bad boss. You create your future by the thoughts you hold today.

The Power of Imaging Our Possibilities
Go confidently in the direction of your dreams.
Live the life you have imagined.
—HENRY DAVID THOREAU

If you still want to go into business after reading the above, I applaud you. This places you in the top ten percent of all people who are leaders. You are an asset to your organization. There are many things you need to know to be successful in business. To advance, you will need tangible and marketable skills to help you grow.

These Are Tools You Will Need to Survive in Business:

<u>Personal</u>
- Positive Self Esteem
- Power Over Your Fears
- Desire To Help Others
- Creativity

<u>Interpersonal Skills</u>
- People Skills/Interpersonal Relationship
- Speaking Skills
- Presentation Skills

<u>Professional Skills</u>
- · Selling Ability
- · Comfort With Change
- · Ability To Balance Empathy and Objectivity
- · Negotiation Skills
- · Leadership

<u>How To Secure Your Business Success</u>
1. Wisdom/Intuition
2. Spiritual Foundation To Handle Adversity

Personal Skills Needed for Success in the Business World

A positive self-esteem will teach you how to: Have respect for yourself and others, have control over one's attitude, how to be polite, think before speaking, avoid rude behavior, avoid being disrespectful to others, curb a "sharp" tongue, how to accept constructive criticism, be less defensive, listen without over reacting, how to cooperate, control a temper, how to be a pleasant person, take the focus off oneself without belittling oneself, and how to avoid arguments. When you have mastery over the above, you will be able to formulate a positive self-esteem, and identity that will help you to succeed financially, socially, spiritually, and morally.

Did you know that **"what you are is God's gift to you, and what you make of your self is your gift to God."**? Start working today on your self-esteem, to make your life a masterpiece worth giving back to God. In the words of President John Fitzgerald Kennedy, "Some people see things as they are and say why? I dream things that never were and say why not?"

Your self-esteem is the thoughts and attitude you hold about yourself. It is the morals and values of your individual and cultural identities. There are five parts to our self-esteem: **Self-Concept, Self-Image, Self-Respect, Self-Worth, Self-Confidence**.

To change or increase your self-esteem, you need to: increase your self-worth, change your self-image from negative to positive, increase your level of self-confidence, and create a business success self-concept (your beliefs). Your self-concept may the most challenging to change, because it is composed of the spoken words, resulting from your thoughts, feelings, your actions, and your experiences.

Your outer world includes all the factors that have gone into your emotional makeup--your inheritance, your infancy, childhood, and teen years. Your outer world consists of all the experiences of your life up to the present. Your experience with the outer world tells one how you were treated, how you were trained and how you related to people the early years of your life. It reflects your parents, family members and the messages they gave to you about yourself, through their facial expressions, tone of voice, attitude, words and actions.

George Herbert Mead, a great social psychologist, uses an interesting phrase to describe a person's relationship to the outer world. He calls it the "looking-glass self." A baby has little concept of the self. But as he grows, he gradually comes to distinguish differences and gain a picture of himself; which is a reflection of the reactions of the important people in his life.

Your self-image is based on a whole system of pictures and feelings you have put together about yourself. It is a combination of imagery, emotions, concepts and feelings.

The three essential components of a healthy self-image are:

0. A sense of belongingness, of being needed and loved. If a child is unwanted, rarely will he have a sense of belonging.
1. Self-Acceptance, an awareness of being wanted, cared for, enjoyed, and loved.
2. Security, be nurtured, cared for, and loved.

The five parts to our self-esteem: **Self-Concept, Self-Image, Self-Respect, Self-Worth, Self-Confidence**.

1. **Self-Concept.** Your self-concept includes mental pictures and emotional feelings. You have a whole system of

feeling-concepts and concept-feelings about yourself. This is at the core of your personality. It is the way you look at and feel about yourself, deep in the heart of your personality. What you see and feel will determine your relationships with other people.

2. **Self-Image**. Self-Image—Inner picture of how you see yourself, reflects outside you. The self you show the world. The self-image evolves continually, according to the situations and experiences you encounter. It is fragile; can be distorted, damaged, or enhanced. Your environment and the people with whom you associate determine how you see yourself.

   You can create a new image any time you desire, by changing your thoughts, feelings and your actions. What we think greatly affects how we feel and how we act. Most people are too lazy, or fear change so they remain the same. We can become comfortable with a bad self-image/self-concept, or a good self-image/self-concept. These are the factors which help you construct or reconstruct your self-image:
   1. Your outer world
   2. Your inner (mental) world
   3. Your spiritual world.

3. **Self-Respect**. Positive self-regard. To like yourself, have a high opinion of yourself as equal to others. If you have little or no respect for the feeling of others; it is because you have experienced emotional hurt by someone. It is the nature of all human beings to be caring and kind. However if you have been treated in an unloving, unkind manner you will become bitter, and develop a hard exterior. Because you are afraid you may get hurt again. An African saying of my moms is, "A burnt child fears fire." When unpleasant things happen to us, it makes us afraid to trust, because we fear the same thing will happen again.

4. **Self-Worth**. A sense of value. Your level of self-worth

depends on your knowledge of who you are, which creates your reality. It is the inner belief and feeling: "I count, I have value, I have something to offer." It is your importance to family, society, life (Higher Power). Everyone is worthy to be alive. You are worthy to be alive or you would not have been created. It may be that you are seeing yourself from a distorted negative view, which needs to be updated. No one is "all bad". To increase your self-worth, identify positive traits or characteristics that set you apart from others. Ask an elderly person, or anyone who has an unbiased opinion of you this question. We all do things sometimes that make us feel ashamed. However we can make amends for the behavior, apologize to the other person and ask them to forgive us.

5. **Self-Confidence.** A sense of being competent. It is the feeling-concept: "I can do this task; I can cope with that situation; I am able to meet life." Put them all together and you have a triad of self-concept feelings: belongingness, worthwhile ness, and Competence. Self-Confidence is self-assured, comfort, an inner peace. It helps you to show courage when confronting a feared area or subject. To act self-assured, without fear, willing to take risks that makes one feel good about oneself. There are three types of persons that tend to destroy your confidence (belief in self). They are Bullies, Manipulators, Braggers, Critics, and Intimidator.

A Positive Self-Esteem is the fuel that keeps you going. You will either fail, or go to great heights in your career, based on your self-esteem. Even if you feel you have a good opinion of yourself it can become eroded by the negative people surrounding you. Your self-esteem is fragile, can be affected by many factors, and needs maintenance on a continual basis.

Through a positive belief in yourself, you can do anything, you decide to do. So begin by saying yes, I can, believe you can do it, then take what ever action necessary to make your idea become a reality.

Equipment

Figure *it out for yourself my friend,*
You've all the greatest of men have had;
two arms, two hands, two legs, two eyes,
And a brain to use if you would be wise.
With this equipment they all began,
So start from the top and say, "I Can."
Look them over, the wise and the great,
They take their food from a common plate,
And similar knives and forks they use,
With similar laces they tie their shoes,
The world considers them brave and smart,
But you've all they had when they made their start.

You can triumph and come to skill,
You can be great if you only will.
You're well equipped for what fight you choose,
You have arms and legs and a brain to use,
And the person who has risen great deeds to do,
Began their life with no more than you.

You are the handicap you must face,
You are the one who must choose your place.
You must say where you want to go,
How much you will study the truth to know;
God has equipped you for life, but He
Lets you decide what you want to be.

Courage must come from the soul within,
The person must furnish the will to win.
So figure it out for yourself my friend,
You were born with all that the great have had,
With your equipment they all began,
So get hold of yourself and say, "I Can." —ANON

Our self-esteem is a state of being, doing, acting, that allows us to appreciate ourselves, and others as valuable and worthwhile. The person with high self-esteem has a positive attitude along with an: I am worthy, I am capable, I am competent, I can do it belief about yourself and life. It is the essence of who you are, not what you or others see you as.

There are many kinds of self-esteem, or beliefs you can hold about yourself. Sometimes they do not carry over or intertwine in all areas of your life. For example your self-esteem in writing reports will not help you in marketing, if you have no skills in selling. Those who work in the self-esteem business say two out of three Americans suffer from low self-esteem. How do you rate?

The following is a Self-Esteem Evaluation Chart by the Barksdale Foundation in Idyllwild, 1974.

Write your answers in your notebook.

Respond to each statement by giving it a rating from 0 to 4, as below:
> **0** – not true any of the time
> **1** – somewhat true or true part of the time
> **2** – fairly true or true about half of the time
> **3** – mainly true or true most of the time
> **4** – true all of the time

1. I do not feel anyone else is better than I am.
2. I am free of shame, blame, guilt and remorse.
3. I am a happy, carefree person.
4. I have no need to prove I am as good or better than others.
5. I do not have a strong need for attention and approval.
6. I do not get upset or feel "less than" when others win.
7. I feel warm and friendly toward myself.
8. I do not feel inferior to anyone who has more or does better than I.

9. I am at ease with strangers and make friends easily.
10. I speak up for my own ideas, likes and dislikes.
11. I am not hurt by others' opinions or attitudes.
12. I do not need praise to feel good about myself.
13. I feel good about others' good fortune.
14. I do not find fault with people.
15. I say "no," even though it may displease other people.
16. I am unafraid to let people see me as I really am.
17. I am friendly, generous and considerate to others.
18. I do not blame others for my problems and mistakes.
19. I enjoy being alone with myself.
20. I accept compliments and gifts without discomfort
    or feeling obligated.
21. I admit my mistakes and defeats without feeling ashamed
    or "less than."
22. I feel no need to defend what I think, say or do.
23. I do not feel "less than" when others tell me I am wrong.
24. I feel intelligent.
25. I do not feel "put down" or "less than" when criticized.

Add up the ratings for your score:
95 or above: You possess sound self-esteem.
Below 90: You are at a disadvantage.
75 or below: You have a serious handicap.
50 or less: You suffer a crippling lack of self-esteem.

Your self-esteem is affected by several things: your self-talk (self-fulfilling prophecy), self-image (dominant picture), external unforeseen controls, and your expectation (performance reality). Your self-talk is critical, because it brings all other factors into play.
Self-Talk ➜ Self-Image ➜ (your dominant picture)
External Controls ➜ Performance Reality.

To be what we are, and to become what we are capable
of becoming, is the only end of life.
—ROBERT LOUIS STEVENSON

The thing that enslaves us to low self-esteem, is our concern over what others do, say, and think about us. And low self-esteem always accompanies low self-confidence. It is a lack of self-confidence that creates the greatest deterrent to one's progress in any new endeavor.

You Maintain A Low Self-Esteem By:
1. Not setting clear goals.
2. Depending upon others for a sense of importance.
3. Not accepting complete responsibility for my life.
4. Depending upon others to do what I need to do.
5. Not differentiating between who I am and what I do.
6. Comparing myself to others and making others a gauge of my importance.
7. Failing to recognize and make choices.
8. Not allowing myself the freedom of expression, the freedom to make mistakes, the freedom to fail.
9. Being fearful and anxious about things I can do nothing about.

The greatest power we have is a made up mind, that we can and will succeed. Belief in oneself and a made up mind is the key to greatness.

Nine Steps To Feel Good About Yourself

1. Do good deeds for others, like opening the door.
2. Treat everyone with respect, and they will do the same for you.
3. Tell people how you feel, tell them what makes you happy or sad.
4. Keep a positive attitude when times are difficult.
5. Treat everyone with respect, and they will treat you the

same way.
6. Seek out people who accept you as you are.
7. Live a healthy life; eat nutritious food and exercise.
8. Stand up for your rights.
9. Listen carefully to what others are saying and try to understand their point of view.

Be Your Own Best Friend

1. A best friend won't condemn you.
2. A best friend will hold you accountable for what you do or not do.
3. A best friend will offer honest feedback.
4. A best friend will support you.
5. A best friend will laugh with you.
6. A best friend will love you when you make a mistake.
7. A best friend will never let you down.
8. A best friend will always believe the best about you.
9. A best friend will always be there for you.
10. A best friend will look for the best in you.

It is wise to frequently take a refresher course to maintain your high level of self-esteem. Mental imagery and visualization can be used, to help you do this or create the job you desire. Let's try it now; first find a quiet spot in your home. Turn off the radio and television; put on loose, comfortable clothing. Now sit down, take in a couple of deep breaths, exhaling slowly, then repeat the process again. Imagine yourself being in a calm peaceful and relaxing place, then bring to mind the position you desire, or image of yourself. If it is a job you want see, in your imagination the location, (street, building, floor), be as specific as you can with the details. See yourself at your new desk. Visualize the dress or suit you will be wearing and the title on your desk. Be sure to visualize your interview with your future boss. See you welcoming and introducing other people who will be working for you. Visualize the salary you desire, flashing across your mind's eye in bold, bright green colors. Money is green, so see lots of fresh, green dollar bills. Do this exercise once a day. Just before you go to bed for 30 days, then once a week for 30 days. Repeat this process until you get the business or whatever it is you desire. Remember to sell yourself at every available opportunity. However, be discreet and use tact. Right timing is very important when you are selling another person on yourself. To do this you will need to conquer all your fears.

Do this mini self-esteem assessment now.
Write your answers in your notebook.
Self-Esteem Assessment

1. Who am I?
2. What makes you special/unique?
3. How did you get to be this way?
4. What makes your ancestry special?
5. Do you have worth?
   A. Are you valuable to society?
   B. How do you convince yourself of this belief?
6. List attributes or talents you possess.
7. How can you acknowledge yourself, without putting others down, who may look or act different from you?
8. What can you do to communicate with others if you are shy or easily embarrassed?
9. List things you can do to like and accept yourself today.
10. What can you do to capitalize on your abilities and talents?
11. Ask yourself, can I financially provide for myself?
    A. What must I do to become financially independent?
    B. What are your 1-year, 5-year, 10-year financial goals?

Your Part
Your good is here. Accept it!
Your joy is near! Embrace it!
Your Power is within. Harness it!
Your victory is now! Claim it!

Your freedom is real. Declare it!
Your abundance is overflowing. Share it!
Your prosperity is good. Receive it!
Your problem is purposeful. Bless it!
Your spirit is divine. Free it!
Your love is great. Give it!
Your faith is mighty. Use it!
—WILLIAM ARTHUR WARD

Power Over Your Fears

All disturbing emotions affect our body in a negative way. Whenever we experience emotions like: doubt, worry, frustration, distrust, anxiety, anger, condemnation, hatred, rage, and fear; the area of light in the cells of our body contracts and shuts off. This prevents the natural in-flow and out-flow of vital cell nutrients needed to maintain the body's inner state of equilibrium. This chemical imbalance affects our immune system, defender against foreign bacteria entry. Then alien, opportunistic bacteria enter the body, disturb its normal homeostasis, to cause cellular break down, and occurrence of disease. We are physical, mental, spiritual beings. Therefore, the foods we eat, the thoughts we think and our inner spiritual state all intertwine to keep us in a state of wholeness and wellness.

Babies have only two fears; the fear of falling and the fear of loud noises. All of our other fears come with knowledge or develop as a result of our experiences, from what we see and hear.

Fear is the most potent toxin and poison to the body and mind. Fear is darkness, the absence of light. When we are afraid, all the light, which is at the center of every cell our body, is blocked off, and unable to be released from the cell, or the body. So we experience darkness from within. Every cell in our body needs to emit light to keep our body in a state of balance.

When we are fearful, all the cells in our body shut down. Nothing can enter or leave the body. When this happens, the body is deprived of the vital nutrients it needs to maintain itself in a state of equilibrium. In this state of imbalance, we are an easy prey for

15

the body to develop disease, and cells of the body to decay and die.

The precursor of fear is doubt. And doubt begets worry, worry begets anxiety, and anxiety creates feelings of: helplessness, hopelessness, despair, futility, depression, unhappiness, lack of peace, lack of contentment, lack of prosperity and abundance, feelings of suicide, destruction of self and mankind.

Physiologically, fear can be measured and quantified as stress or disease in the body. Fear can alter our life style and life span. Fear is the precipitating factor that causes individuals and countries to war against each other. It is the basis of all bias, prejudice, discrimination, and isolationism. Fear is the underlying emotion when people commit violent acts of aggression against each other. Fear underlies neurotic and psychotic emotional breakdowns in the personality. It prevents the development of love, and intimacy in personal relationships.

There is an interrelationship between our emotions and our body. We need to understand that our world of experiences and bodily functions is part of the eternal divine flow of life. All negative emotions produce a toxin that is poisonous to our body's cells. Therefore, the negative emotions we hold about ourselves and others affect us on a deep cellular level. They can shorten our life span and negatively impact our quality of life.

Our body's energy can be likened to the energy of a fire. A fire generates heat, light, movement, and action. The amount of fire/energy we have is in direct proportion to the passionate drive of our inner life force. Our life's mission gives us a feeling of purpose and a path to follow in life. Our inner life force is determined by the energy vibrations of the cells of our body. The amount of fire/energy we radiate from the cells of our body is the result of our level of aliveness or excitement about living, our ability to cope with the challenges we confront each day. Most of the fears on which we dwell daily are negative, non-productive energy depletes, rather than life giving, "light," energy sustainers.

Our fears rob us of energy, stamina and the drive we need to handle our tasks of daily living. A lack of energy can cause us to be lethargic, procrastinate, act indifferent, and behave in a depressed, down mood. We were created to enjoy life and the fruits of our labor; "For God hath not given us a spirit of fear, but of power, love, and a sound mind." We need courage to conquer our fears. *We were born with and possess a spirit of courage, not a spirit of timidity and fear.*

Affirmation

If I am feeling a bit low, I remind myself of the truth that I am an important person and necessary part of life. I let go feelings of insecurity, low self-worth, and realize I am a child of God, living in love, and doing everything I can to create a happier atmosphere for myself and others.

Our fears keep us in darkness and prevent us from letting our "light-energy" shine through. The fears that handicap us the most are: *Fear of change, fear of rejection, fear of power, fear of success, fear of money, fear of failure, fear of responsibility, fear of criticism, fear of ill health/old age, fear of death, fear of expression, fear of enjoying life, fear of the unknown (problems that may not occur), fear of being happy.*

Fear is the enemy of love, joy, peace, happiness, contentment, and faith. And where there is no faith, there is no spiritual development. And where there is no spiritual development, there is no God. And where there is no God, we feel abandoned, unloved, unwanted, and alone.

When we are loved we get a warm glow of light about us and we feel a sensation of warmth and love. When we are full of light, the darkness disappears from our body, mind, and soul (spirit). The brighter the light within us, the greater is the fire. Our fire gives us the energy and drive we need to accomplish our daily tasks.

The light and fire inside us is waiting to get out, to radiate throughout our body and the universe. What we send out returns to us. To feel the light and love of our Divine self, we need to master fear. We have to move through our fears to light the fire within us.

Our fears are the barriers that hold us back and keep us locked

17

into nonproductive behaviors, activities, and relationships. When we experience thoughts of fear, everything in our world appears to be out of focus. The mental image sent out may be clear, but our mind picks up and distorts the image. As we move through our fears, we light the fire within us.

We are beings of light. We have a physical and a spiritual body of light. At the center of each cell in our body is an area of light. Therefore, we are a body of light.

When we are frightened or fearful, a torrent of powerful chemicals, adrenaline, and acetylcholine, are released from the cells of our body and mind, to paralyze, and render them useless to function as normal.

Due to conditioning our fears act as a barrier and keeps us locked into nonproductive behaviors, activities, and relationships. When we experience thoughts of fear, everything in our mental world and emotional world is non-focused. Then the mental images sent to the mind are unclear and distorted due to prior conditioning.

As we move through our fears, we let go confusion, negativity, and emotional trauma of the past. As you develop spiritually, you begin to feel your oneness with God. When you know you are one with God; your spiritual awareness helps you eliminate worry, doubt, anxiety, resentment, anger, revenge, jealousy, envy, and fear. Then you feel an inner contentment, peace, harmony, joy, happiness, and love which ignites the fire (enthusiasm) within you. Why not do it now!

Do It Now

Until one is committed, there is hesitancy, the chance to draw back, always ineffectiveness.
Concerning all acts of initiative, there is one elementary truth the ignorance of which kills countless ideas and splendid plans: That the moment one definitely commits oneself, then providence moves too. All sorts of things occur to help one that would never otherwise have occurred.

A whole stream of events issues from the decision, raising in one's favor all manner of unforeseen incidents and meetings and material assistance which no man could have dreamed would have come his way. What ever you can do, or dream you can, begin it. Boldness has genius, power, and magic in it. Begin it now
—GOETHE

Fear of Success. To achieve success, we must believe that success can happen, that it can happen for anyone, and that it will happen for us. Most of our energy is used in a destructive manner to dwell on what we fear may happen. Our mind creates through our mental impressions. It will create whatever our mental energy presents to it. If our thoughts are focused on what we fear may happen, or on what we fear may never happen, our mind will create it. Your fears are borne from the dark imagining in your mind thinking of what could possibly occur. To avoid getting into the habit of a fear reaction, still your mind, focus on *what could be*, rather than on what is taking place in your life now.

Know that God wants you to reach your goals. Your dreams are the divine thought seeds planted in your mind by God to help you have a larger experience of your divinity. The infinite intelligence of God needs you as an expression of "Itself." Know that all of life wants you to be a success.

Often your fear of being successful will have its origin in one of the following areas, a fear:
1. To exceed family members or family expectations of success.
2. Non-acceptance by the individual and parent/s of what behavior to expect from the successful person.
3. Fear one's (parents) may reject them, because the parent fears the child may reject them.
4. The parent/s may feel uncomfortable relating to the successful child due to their feelings of inferiority/inadequacy.

A Fear of Money manifests as *lack and limitation*. Because we fear having money, we may act irresponsibly; squander or misuse

19

it. We must respect money, for it has an energy vibration of its own. Money will not remain where it is not respected and appreciated. Also, you cannot hold negative thoughts about money or the people who possess it. *God made everything good, including money.*

Money is not bad, it is the love (worship) of money that gives us trouble. You cannot make a god out of money. Money is a necessary commodity to purchase goods and supplies for our daily needs. However, we must employ self-discipline and use good judgment as we accumulate and dispense money. Do not try to hold onto or hoard money. Money is energy, and energy circulates continually. It is never stagnant.

Remember, you do not get money from God, but rather avenues of expression through which the substance of money flows to you as creative ideas.

Charles P. Conn states in his book, *Making It Happen* (A Christian looks at money, competition, and success), that "Hard work for financial gain is expected of us (by God) and not to be discouraged. And he cites several Bible references to support his statement: "All hard work brings a profit, but mere talk leads only to poverty. Proverb 14:23 NIV. The plans of the diligent lead to profit as surely as haste leads to poverty. Proverb 21:5 NIV. Lazy hands make a man poor, but diligent hands bring wealth. Proverb 10:4 NIV."

The amount of money you have for your use is based on your self-esteem, which is based on the belief that you are one of a kind, created in the image and likeness of a loving, perfect God. It is done unto you, as you believe. What you mentally see is what you will produce. Jesus stated, "If ye have faith as a grain of mustard seed, ye shall say unto this mountain, remove hence to yonder place, and it shall move, and nothing shall be impossible to you." Most of us do not have a positive belief in goodness, justice, and right action. This causes us to be enslaved to our fears, worries, and doubts about our livelihood. Hard work for financial gain is expected of us and is not to be discouraged.

*All hard work brings a profit, but mere talk leads only to
poverty.* —PROVERBS 14:23 NIV

*The plans of the diligent lead to profit as surely as haste
leads to poverty.* —PROVERBS 21:5 NIV

*Lazy hands make a man poor, but diligent hands bring
wealth.* —PROVERBS 10:4 NIV

The World of Manifestation

Your mind is creative. It creates everything from the thoughts you
think, so use your mental creative skills to create what you want to
occur in your life. Your present physical world is the result of
thoughts you have held over the years. Your yesterday thoughts are
your today experiences. To create anything new, you must change
your: thoughts, spoken word, feelings, actions/no action (reactions)
To manifest your desires, or create a success image: Sit for 5
minutes with your eyes closed in a calm and quiet state, then
contemplate yourself from your highest point of view.

Money is neither good nor bad, it can be used for good and
evil. It is a person's thinking about money, and use of it that causes
problems. Jack Addington states in his book, *The Secrets Of
Prosperity*, that there is a law of life that guarantees us as much
prosperity as we can accept for our selves and we are willing to
receive through giving of ourselves into life.

Poverty is a belief in lack, or want; a belief that man has to
make his prosperity happen because it depends upon outer
conditions or circumstances. Poverty is a sin that must be
overcome if man is to share in the fullness of God or enjoy the
abundant life." We must learn and accept that God is the source of
our supply, therefore our supply is infinite. Besides, there is
nothing in the Bible that says poverty is a virtue. The Bible does
speak of money; it indicates that money should not be worshipped
or shunned. Affirm now:

God is my infinite source of supply, and this supply is within me right now. God has planted His spirit inside us, therefore God is always with us, He waits for our acknowledgement and recognition.

Faith is a positive belief in what we want to experience, and fear is a negative belief in what we do not want to experience. Both are states of belief. Our mind can not occupy two states of an opposing belief at a time. We will either believe in a positive outcome (faith) about money and money substance, or we will think on and visualize a negative outcome about money. Our belief about money is based on our learned irrational fears. Use the following strategies to help you develop a prosperity consciousness.

1. Develop an inner knowing of your divine and unlimited potential. Accept God as your willing partner to provide all your needs. This will require faith and belief in a power that cannot be seen through the physical eye. Jesus said, "All things are possible to him that believeth." Mark: 23 Do you have this faith?
2. Ask yourself what is your divine purpose for being on earth? All human beings were created to produce and prosper. Life is a reciprocal process. It is about giving and receiving. When you can clearly understand how prosperity benefits your life's purpose to survive on the planet, it will unfold naturally for you.
3. Define with clarity why you want to be prosperous. What is it that you would love to be, do, or have? What is it you desire to manifest into your experience that would benefit you while enriching the life of your fellow man? Do you want more money to provide security and material pleasures for your loved ones? Write down your desires now on paper. Be specific and give descriptive details of why you need the money, and what you will do with the money once you get it.
4. How will your having money benefit mankind? Allow

your imagination to soar and imagine how your life would change positively if you had this money. We really can have all we desire. But having it all means more than material wealth, career success, or loving relationships. We will need to grow spiritually to develop an unshakable faith in God before we can have all we desire. It will require that we develop patience, a tolerance for ambiguity, change, letting go of control, so you are able to listen to the quiet and still voice within, as it dictates the direction and path you must take to have what you desire.

One way to take constructive action to dispel anxiety about money matters, is to become knowledgeable through the services of a financial planner. A person who doesn't have a lot of money, can start investing a small amount in a money market fund, and add to it each month. A long-term investment would be to set aside money monthly in an IRA (Individual Retirement Annuity) plan. You can always buy savings bonds, in denominations of twenty-five dollars, fifty dollars or more. Start your own savings account independently, or keep ten dollars each month in your checking account that you do not touch until Christmas. There is an association of African American Financial Planners who offer a free 30-minute consultation to help you set goals and strategies. Help is available, but you must seek it. It does not matter what you do, just do something to change your financial picture from bleak to rosy.

Write your answers in your notebook.

1. My goals in the following areas are:
<u>Personal</u>:

      A. One year goal
      B. Five year goal
      C. Ten year goal

<u>Professional</u>:
    A. One year goal
    B. Five year goal
    C. Ten year goal
<u>Spiritual</u>:
    A. One year goal
    B. Five year goal
    C. Ten year goal
<u>Social</u>:
    A. One year goal
    B. Five year goal
    C. Ten year goal

What beliefs do you hold, that block your personal, professional, social, or spiritual growth?

2. My 1-year, 5-year, and 10-year goals in the following areas are: Write a **month and year** when you plan to achieve **each goal**

Career Goals –
Relationships –
Social Goals –

A Prosperity Affirmation

I am prosperous. I never entertain thoughts of poverty or lack.
I am supplied from the Infinite Source with all that I need
    and to spare.
Right ideas come to me when I need them.
I make right decisions at the right time.
I am never alone. I have a Silent Partner who works with me
    in everything I do. He is within me, working with me each
    moment of the day.
I have no regrets for the past, no fear for this moment, nor any
    anxiety for the future. I am protected by an Infinite Power;

*I am guided by Divine Intelligence and I am sustained by
a Loving Presence. All is well and I am thankful.*
—JACK ADDINGTON

Prosperity Affirmation
*My good is never taken away from me, because I am dealing with
an Infinite supply. Loss is out of my consciousness. What is mine
by Divine Right I cannot lose, I open the door to the opportunities
that await me today.*
—DR. FRANK RICHELIEU "THE PROSPERITY CONNECTION"

Fear of Failure is an expectation and concentration on what we
don't want to happen; fearing the worst brings it about. Failure is a
state of mind that is created through our imagination; therefore, it
is a relative and subjective state.

To create anything new, requires you to change your behavior.
Change is not easy for any of us. Usually we resist change because
we are unable to project our desire into the future, to see a positive
outcome. All growth-mental, emotional and spiritual-requires that
we let go of old beliefs and habits.

Jesus said that we could not put new wine into an old bottle.
Likewise, we cannot create new behavior from an old behavioral
pattern. For the new behavior will be contaminated by the old. To
make lasting changes in the creation of a new behavior requires
you to let go the old to make room for the new behavior. This is
also true if you want to make a positive change in your lifestyle.
You have to let go the old to make room for the new.

Prayer Treatment To Control Fear

*With God's help I am in control. My fears subside and the cause
of them passes. They were never the truth. Fear is only a false
illusion appearing as real. God's love is the truth and only
power, and it is protecting me now. I have absolute peace of
mind. Peace like a river is cleansing me of fear right now.
A circle of Light surrounds me, and nothing of harm can enter my*

physical, mental, or spiritual world. I am guided into right action and clear thinking. Only love goes from me and only love returns to me. Thank you, Father, Mother, God; you are all I need.

Fear of Responsibility can take the form of helplessness, being or acting like a victim, emotional/mental blocking, or an unwillingness to act on our own behalf. Our spiritual growth may require that we experience pain, as well as pleasure, along life's way. Each of us has a different spiritual path to follow because our emotional weaknesses and character development are not the same. Some of us may need to grow in patience, while others may need to learn to be honest in business transactions, overcome greed, envy, or jealousy. The spiritual path of growth will be different for each of us. Therefore it is unwise to mimic or follow the lead of another.

We are all on an individual spiritual journey through life. Our spiritual path may intersect that of many people; however, that does not mean we must or should walk in their footsteps. Each of us must carve out the divine road map that lies before us. No one can travel the road of life for us, even though it might be an act of unselfish love. We each must meet God face to face, to be aware of the powerful presence that controls the universe and allows us to enjoy the fruits of life (joy, peace, contentment, happiness, and bliss). We are here on the planet to serve mankind. We are all interconnected. What affects one, affects all. We have a personal and moral responsibility to be our best. According to Mahatma Gandhi, "There are seven sins in the world: Wealth without work; knowledge without character; science without humanity; worship without sacrifice; politics without principle; commerce without morality; pleasure without conscience." Ask yourself if you are ready for business success?

Self Test
Am I Ready For Business Success?

Answer **Yes** or **No** to each question

Write your answers in your notebook.

1. I know what I want out of life?
2. Have I chosen a business that blends with my personality, abilities and interests?
3. I know my business strengths and weaknesses and I have taken measures to utilize the services and skills of others to balance my weaknesses.
4. I have accepted that I will need the services of competent professional for my business growth and I am prepared to pay for these services.
5. Do you have financial and quantitative goals set for yourself and your business?
6. Do you have an action plan for accomplishing your goals and are they tied to a time frame?
7. Are you self-disciplined?
8. Can you work long hours and make sacrifices?
9. Do you have management ability?
10. Do you have enough experience in your field?
11. Are your goals realistic and obtainable?
12. Do you love what you do?
13. Is your purpose to own a business clear to you?

Write your assessment of yourself in your notebook.

The best way to avoid fear is to organize your mind and life. And the best way to get control over your daily affairs is to have a daily "To Do List" and use it. Below is a sample to get you get organized.

Things To Do Today

Write your list in your notebook.

Date   Completed Y/N

1...

2...

3...

etc.

Desire To Help Others

Abraham Maslow is credited with identifying the basic needs of all people, they are:

- Physiological Needs, (hunger, thirst, sex, sleep, exercise, rest, air to breathe)
- Safety Needs (physical-shelter, protection, and psychological order, spiritual meaning)
- Belongingness and Love Needs
- Esteem Needs
- Self-Actualization or Self-Fulfillment

Our needs arrange themselves in a hierarchical order of importance. So that our higher needs will only be satisfied after our lower needs are met. Therefore we are motivated by our unmet needs. You will be able to better focus on the needs of others after your basic needs have been met. Often times our desire to help others is an attempt to satisfy one of our unfulfilled needs. Study yourself to understand your underlying motivation. So that you are a helper rather than an enabler.

When we try to meet our needs through helping others, we send a dual message and we also function in a dual role. We may verbally say you are the most important person in my life but behavioral say I am the most important person in my world. It is the highest order in the universe for us to help another person.

However, we cannot give water from an empty bucket. So take time to attend your needs first, so you can be fully present and available in the giving of yourself to others.

We can give of ourselves in many ways. Nikki Giovanni says, "There is always something to do. There are hungry people to feed, naked people to clothe, sick people to comfort and make well. And while I don't expect you to save the world I do think it's not asking too much for you to love those with whom you sleep, share the happiness of those whom you call friend, engage those among you who are visionary and remove from your life those who offer you depression, despair, and disrespect."

In his book *The Prophet*, Kahlil Gibran has this to say On Giving:

> *Then said a rich man, speak to us of Giving. And he answered:*
> *You give but little when you give of your possessions.*
> *It is when you give of yourself that you truly give.*
> *For what are your possessions but things you keep and guard*
> *   for fear you may need tomorrow?*
> *And tomorrow what shall tomorrow bring to the over prudent*
> *   dog burying bones in the trackless sand as he follows the*
> *   pilgrims to the holy city?*
> *And what is fear of need but need itself?*
> *Is not dread of thirst when your well is full, the thirst that is*
> *   unquenchable?*
> *There are those who give little of the much which they have-*
> *   and they give it for recognition and their hidden desire*
> *   makes their gifts unwholesome.*
> *and there are those who have little and give it all.*
> *These are the believers in life and the bounty of life and their*
> *   coffer is never empty.*
> *There are those who give with joy and that joy is their reward.*
> *And there are those who give with pain and that pain is their*
> *   baptism.*

*And there are those who give and know not pain in giving, nor
do they seek job, nor give with mindfulness of virtue.
They give as in yonder valley the myrrh breathes Its fragrance
into space.
Through the hands of such as these God speaks, and from
behind their eyes He smiles upon the earth.*

*It is well to give when asked, but it is better to give unasked,
understanding; and to the open-handed the search for one
who shall receive is joy greater than giving.
And is there aught you would behold?
All you have shall some day be given; therefore, give now, that
the season of giving may be yours and not your inheritors'.*

*You often say, "I would give, but only to the deserving."
The trees in your orchard say not so, nor the flocks in your
pasture.
They give that they may live, for to withhold is to perish.
Surely he who is worthy to receive his days and his nights is
worthy of all else from you.*

*And he who has deserved to drink from the ocean of life
deserves to fill his cup from your little stream.
And what desert greater shall there be, than that which lies in
the courage and the confidence, nay the charity, of
receiving.*

This poem reminds us we are all interconnected. There is a spirit inside
us that urges us to reach out and touch another person. People can be
unreasonable, illogical, and self-centered, but we must love them
anyway. Give and it will be given unto you pressed down and
overflowing. No one has enough talents to do everything well, this why
we need the help and cooperation of others. Charles Paul Conn states it
well in his Principle of Inclusion, "One of the best-kept secrets in life is
that including other people in one's goals lends energy and impetus to
reaching the goals themselves. The truth is that people who achieve

greatly usually *share* greatly." He says there are two kinds of people in the world, excluders and includers. And big achievers are big includers, which of these are you? How?

Daily Guide to Happiness

Pray: It is the greatest power on earth.
Read: It is the fountain of wisdom.
Think: It is the source of power.
Give: It is too short a day to be stingy.
Save: It is the secret of security.
Play: It is the secret of perpetual youth.
Work: It is the price of success.
Laugh: It is the music of the soul.
Love: It is the road to happiness.
Be Caring: It is a God given privilege.
   —NORMAN VINCENT PEALE

The Joys Of Giving

To be a friend a person should go more than halfway with their fellowman, they should greet others first and not wait to be greeted; and radiate a spirit of overflowing good will.

To be a friend a person should remember that we are human magnets; that like attracts like, and that what we give we get.

To be a friend a person should recognize that no one knows all the answers, and that we should add each day to our knowledge of how to live the friendly way.
   —WILFORD PETERSON/ADAPTED BY IDA GREENE

Purpose, A Reason For Living

Purpose gives meaning to life. Purpose gives Joy and
 Zest to living.
What is your Desire, your Dream? When our eye is on our

goal, we are not easily disturbed by things around us
Our purpose awakens new trains of thoughts in our mind.
Our purpose directs these trains of thought into new fields of
*   achievement.*
To succeed in life we must have some great purpose in mind;
*   some goal toward which we would like to achieve.*
Find a purpose, today.

—ANON

Creativity
Our world of experiences is created through our mind, by the thoughts we think on a continual basis. A thought is an unspoken word, a word is a spoken thought, and a behavior is a thought and word that is acted out. I define creativity as risk taking behavior, without fear, utilizing problem-solving skills.

You will need to be very creative to know when to make the right moves that will move you forward on your career path. Since the brain is the seat of creativity, lets understand how it works.

The brain is divide into two hemispheres, the left hemisphere, which deals with logical/linear thinking, it is objective, and rational. The left hemisphere of the brain handles convergent thinking. It helps us get closure with issues. It answers questions of when and where. Yet another area of the left hemisphere helps us with reasoning or <u>deductive thinking</u>.

1. <u>Deductive thinking moves from a general to specific focus</u> to arrive at a conclusion. The right side of the brain deals with creativity. It is creative/explorative thinking (testing, analyzing, processing data).
2. <u>Inductive thinking goes from the specific to general</u> to arrive at a conclusion.
3. Concentration skill is a deep focus of the brain to increase recall or memory of information you desire to learn.
4. Investigative thinking searches into, explores, or examines closely with a desire to find something new in addition to what you already know. And it expends the effort to find out the unknown.

5. Visualization — The ability to create a mental picture from a thought, a picture in mind without sound, or restructure a thought pattern.
6. Problem Solving — Brainstorm (unrestricted flow of Ideas), define problem, analyze, attack, accept solution.
7. Socratic Method — Look for fallacies in evidence, reasoning, language; why?
8. Divergent Thinking moves in different directions. It asks the questions who, what, when, how? It allows you to take a step back to view all parts of the situation; here you detach yourself from the problem. When you relax the conscious mind it frees up the subconscious mind, the seat of creativity.
9. Lateral Thinking solves problem in an indirect way by asking the questions — is it useable? Does it work?
10. Critical thinking skills engages both right and left hemispheres of the brain. It finds the implications of facts and principles. It is the ability to see concepts and principles, which underlie or are implicit in all data. And discovers new relation or relationships. *It uses the Socratic method, and examines issues from different perspectives; using all the senses to arrive at a conclusion. By focusing on end result and what one wants to achieve.*

To engage your brain in critical thinking, do the following exercises:

1. Combine verbal, visual, and kinesthetic facts to form a diverse image.
2. Add emotional content to the image e.g. humor, sense of importance etc.
3. Associate an idea with other ideas you already remember, so that recalling the ideas or word elicits the new idea.

In the words of Dr. Benjamin Mays, "It is not your environment; It is not your history; It is not your education or ability; It is the quality of your mind that predicts your future." So care enough about yourself to take time to develop your mind.

The values you hold tell the story of your life. And these same values will allow you to be creative or restrictive.

Because they reflect the real you. *In your notebook* write down, from the list below, the values that apply to you. Then write down the ones you would like to have. Underline those which you feel are essential for business success.

Values

- **Recognition:** getting respect, prestige, and social approval.
- **Achievement:** attaining mastery of a field, self-advancement, and growth.
- **Leadership:** directing, having power and influence over others.
- **Social Service:** doing something that has a benefit for others.
- **Self-expression:** working in an area suited to your abilities.
- **High Income:** gain in socio-economic status, meeting material needs.
- **Work Ethic:** belief one must work in order to be a useful member of society.
- **Independence:** being free from supervision and restriction.
- **Creativity:** contributing new ideas, be original and inventive.
- **Challenge:** handling difficult or complex work.
- **Interpersonal Relations:** interacting with other employees.
- **Variety:** preferring diverse activities.
- **Interest:** finding a stimulating activity.
- **Security:** certainty of having a job and an income.

Learn how to use your critical thinking skills to problem solve and cope with bothersome emotions. Critical thinking uses risk taking behaviors which requires you to use your ingenuity and creativity; because it demands determination and effort on your part. Here are examples of some problems you might encounter in your work environment:

Write your comments in your notebook.

1. Male dominated company that uses "old boy standards" to move up in the corporation. You are stuck at a certain level and can't seem to get promoted. Do you file a grievance with the labor relations department? Do you file a grievance with the Equal Employment Opportunity Commission, or do you try to get a good evaluation and seek employment at a more progressive firm. How you respond will have a lot to do with your goals.

   Are you a female trying to change company policies of discrimination towards females? If your goal is to move ahead as swift as possible, you may make waves. Even if you transfer out of the corporation, how do you know if you will receive a favorable recommendation? You may be given a formal letter of recommendation to take with you, and have an unfavorable phone call precede you. You will need to use your creative abilities to ascertain what course of action to take. Take a moment and write on a separate piece of paper how you would handle these issues.

2. Luncheon, business meeting, social engagement; you are new on the job! You are invited by your boss to all of the above. Should you accept all three invitations or decline all three. *Write your comments in your notebook.*

   Until you know the rules of the corporation, you are safer attending a meeting where business matters are to be discussed. Always keep your goals before you; know why are you there in the corporation.

3. Do you know the rules of your corporation? What is the office politics? Do you have to play politics to move up in the corporation? What have others before you done to get promoted? Are there cliques in the organization? Do you need to be a part of one? If so, which one leads to advancement? If you are female, how have other females advanced in the corporation? Is it a practice to have a non-business relationship with the boss to get promoted? Do you know what are the

formal and informal rules of a corporation? Who are the "in group" (movers) and which is the "out group" (watchers and gossipers). *Write your comments in your notebook.*

There are no hard rules to follow, as when to take a risk, and when not to. But if you rely on your intuition, you will seldom go wrong. Remember, if you get fired it is not the end of the world. Sometimes you need to let go of something to discover what you don't want. Whenever you engage in risk taking behavior without fear, it shows that you know how to use power and is not afraid of it. What did you learn from these exercises?

Write your comments in your notebook.

People who succeed differ greatly from those who fail.

Because what we believe to be true, becomes true. What do you believe about yourself, is it good, bad or indifferent?

Beliefs Activity
In your notebook:
1. List 5 key beliefs that have limited you in the past.
2. List 3 positive beliefs that can serve to support you in achieving your highest goals.

Man Is What He Believes
—ANTON CHEKHOV

Chapter 2

Interpersonal Skills Needed
For Business Success

People Skills/Interpersonal Relationship

It is our concern over what others say, do and think about us that enslaves our mind, our body, and our spirit. We are always communicating to others through our words and our behavior.

Communication is the use of words signals, gestures, body language, or any expressive behavior we show that is interpreted by another person, has meaning to them, that they understand, or recognize from their past associations.

Interpersonal communication is a form of verbal expression between people about what they desire, wish, doubt or fear. We bring to ourselves in the same communication anything we desire, fear, or hate.

Inner personal communication is self talk (thoughts, emotions) to the self about one's goals, desires, wishes, doubts, fears, or anxieties. We communicate our feelings, and ideas needs in a manner which ensures they will be heard. Also we accept, believe, and feel we will be heard. If we are heard incorrectly it is because our signals are unclear, the receiver was unable to receive the message we sent, or we sent a confusing or mixed message.

The forms of communication are:
· Written communication
· Verbal communication
· Media — Visual arts, graphic arts, Television
· Technical — Computers
· Expressive — Drama, Theater, Ballet, Music
· Inner Personal Communication

Effective communication identifies, and describes the action you desire, and ignores the motive. It controls fear and anxiety by control of the breath through your jaw, and mouth movement.

To communicate effectively specify what you want, request small changes in behavior specify what behavior you are willing to change to reach an agreement with the person you desire to influence. Other things you can do to communicate better are to: Be cooperative, show the other person you want to reach a compromise. Be tolerant of the other person's imperfections, express your feelings calmly, try to incorporate caring in your voice when speaking, pay attention to your tone of voice and its pitch, be pleasant, act friendly, and have a positive attitude.

Assumptions and Skills For Effective Communication

1. The first basic assumption is that feelings, all kinds, **EXIST**. They are neither good nor bad, right nor wrong, correct nor incorrect—they just **ARE**.
2. The second assumption is that all of us have the right to have any feeling in the world. Some behaviors or actions may need to be limited, but any feeling is okay. And each of us is the ultimate authority on our own feelings.

   No one can tell you what you feel or don't feel. Another person may not like what you are feeling or may feel differently. But no one can tell you that you don't feel the way that you do.
3. The third assumption is that an intimate relationship, is a place where both partners feel safe to share feelings, when they choose to, without getting attacked for it.

You need two sets of communication skills. One set is for speaking, and one is for listening. Both skills are essential.

Skills for Speaking. Use "I-messages." An "I-message" is a sentence that starts with the word "I" and expresses a feeling. Here is why a "I-message" is more effective than a "you-message." Suppose X says to Y, "You play too much golf." Y can protest, "I do not." Y feels attacked and put down and may be tempted to retaliate with a counterattack. But if X says to Y, "I feel jealous when you play golf," Y cannot say, "You do not." X is taking responsibility for his or her own feelings, and no one can say that X doesn't, or shouldn't, feel that way.

To communicate what you are feeling, you need to know what you are feeling. This takes practice. It involves getting to know your body and the signals it gives to tell you what you are feeling. It also involves becoming familiar with the pattern of thoughts that go along with specific feelings for you.

Positive Feelings

relaxed	willing	content	turned on
calm	secure	loving	ready
sexy	happy	peaceful	ambitious
excited	busy	confident	imaginative
warm	strong	bubbly	interested

Negative Feelings

grouchy	ashamed	silly	sorry
sad	bored	hurt	incompetent
anxious	alone	shy	rebellious
tired	dumb	guilty	confused
nervous	trapped	frustrated	listless
restless	put down	defensive	depressed

In active listening we communicate our feelings, ideas, and needs in a manner which ensure so that we will be heard. We accept, believe and know that we will be heard. If we are heard incorrectly, it is because our signals were unclear, the receiver was unable to receive our message, or we sent a mixed message.

The 20 verbs listed below describe some ways people feel and act sometimes. Think of your behavior in interaction with other people. How do you feel and act with other people? _Write in your notebook_ the five verbs which best describe your behavior in interaction with others.

acquiesces	disapproves
advises	evades
agrees	initiates
analyzes	judges
assists	leads
concedes	obliges
cooperates	relinquishes
coordinates	resists
criticizes	retreats
directs	withdraws

Ineffective communication that is unresolved creates a fertile environment for stress. We can become stressed because we are afraid to communicate. We fear our attempt to communicate may be ignored, misinterpreted, or used as a tool to work against us by the other person. Other causes of ineffective communication are: Impaired hearing, poor vision, speech problems, mental confusion, negative emotions resulting from anger, criticism, low self-esteem, jealousy, and rage.

Unresolved inner personal conflict or interpersonal conflict will manifest as stress. Stress is a behavioral outlet of unresolved inner personal or interpersonal issues. Everything we think, say or do has a consequence in our lives. The U.S. Center for Disease Control estimates that 51.5% of all deaths of people under the age of 65 is attributed to unhealthy behaviors and lifestyle. To have more effective communication reduce your stress by doing the following:

1. Acknowledge when you are stressed.
2. Make a conscious decision to stop your stress cycle.
3. Remind yourself that you are in control.
4. Be 100 percent committed to resolve the source of your stress. Seek to find a solution.
5. Take a deep breath release physical and mental tension as you exhale.
6. When appropriate leave the stressful situation.

7. Break the stress cycle, focus your mind on a positive thought, play relaxing music, a motivational tape or smile.
8. Take a break, close your eyes, allow your emotions to arise and release them out of your mind. Don't accept your thoughts and don't reject them.
9. Don't blame, pity, or punish yourself or anyone else.
10. Think about the positive growth or opportunities resulting from this situation.

Cognitive Approaches To Managing Stress

Write your answers and comments in your notebook

Reaction Assessment
1. Do I have all the facts?   Yes/No
       What are the facts?
2. Is there anything I can do about this situation or is it beyond my control?   Yes/No
3. Am I able to stand back and view this situation clearly and objectively?   Yes/No
4. What is the worst thing that could happen to me?
5. Is my thinking unclear, affected or influenced by an accumulation of chain of stressful events? Yes/No
6. Am I expending more energy on this situation than its worth?   Yes/No
       In what way?
7. How could I have responded differently or more effectively?

Response Assessment To Questions Above
    1. Totally affected — flight or flight response
    2. Mildly affected — but not acting upon it
    3. Not affected — you are detached
        If you can't fight or flee—FLOW—let it go

List 15 Feelings You Have About Relationships
Write out three incidences in communicating with others you find upsetting, and wish you could handle differently. Choose recent

situations that you would like to see a positive change. This includes the possibility that a change may occur for you whether the other person changes or not.

Use the format of briefly describing the situation, what you <u>felt</u> when you were upset, the <u>outcome</u> you wanted, <u>if it occurred</u> how you would have felt about yourself and the other person.

Write your answers and comments in your notebook

Situation #1:
Situation #2:
Situation #3:

Understanding Ourselves
Each Other And Your Profession

Write your answers and comments in your notebook

- What Are Some Of Your Unfulfilled Past Expectations/Dreams/Fantasies
- My Current Realities Are:
- Some Major Disappointments For Me Are:
- My Present Hopes Or Future Wishes Are:

One of the greatest joys in life comes from the relationships we form with others. Susan Smith Jones, Ph.D. states that *"We Create Lasting Relationships* by **Being** the *Right Person*, **Not** *Finding the Right Person.*" Are you the *Right Person* or, are you desperately trying to **Find** the *Right Person* in life. Answer the following questions below to better understand your relationship to yourself and others.

Your Relationship to Yourself

Write your answers or comments in your notebook

1. Who am I?
2. What am I?
3. Do I make sense to others?

4. Am I worthwhile?
5. Why am I alive?
6. Do I have a personal relationship to life? It is:
7. Do I love myself?   Why? Do I love people?

Your Relationship to Others

Write your answers or comments in your notebook

1. Am I wanted?
2. Am I needed?
3. Am I loved? By whom?
4. Do I belong?
5. Can I trust people?
6. Do I have affection for myself/people?
7. Do I express my affection?
8. Do I fear rejection? If so, why?
9. Do I believe in a Supreme Power?
11. Is there a God?
12. Does God love me?
13. What is God to me?
14. What is my relationship to God?
15. What is my relationship to the Universe?
16. Is life for or against me?

There are many gifts we can give, but the greatest gift we can give another human being is the gift of love. There is no limit to the amount of love we can give or to the forms that love can take. We do this by extending kind gestures to others, speak encouraging words, listening quietly when words are not needed, calling on the phone to inquire about the persons welfare, sending a card, or showing we care in our own special way. Whenever we give our love freely, it returns to us abundantly. Loving and genuine concern is the key to dynamic interpersonal relations. Lets look at relationships in your life.

Relationships In My Life

Write your answers and comments in your notebook

1. As a friend, the things I like best about myself are…
2. As a friend, the things I like least about myself are…
3. My rewards for having close friends are…
4. My rewards for having few or no close friends are…
5. I prevent myself from making new friends by…
6. I prevent myself from turning acquaintances into intimate friends by…
7. I reject offers of friendship/ opportunities for new friendships by…
8. In losing my friendship with…(name someone who is no longer a friend) I take responsibility for:

Class

Class never runs scared. It is surefooted and confident. It can handle whatever comes along.

Class has a sense of humor. It knows that a good laugh is the best lubricant for oiling the machinery of human relations.

Class never makes excuses. It takes its lumps and learns from past mistakes. Class knows that good manners are nothing more than a series of petty sacrifices.

Class bespeaks an aristocracy that has nothing to do with money. Some extremely wealthy people have no class at all while others who are struggling to make ends meet are loaded with it.

Class is real. You can't fake it. The person with class makes everyone feel comfortable because they are comfortable with themselves.

If you have class you've got it made. If you don't have class, no matter what else you have, it doesn't make any difference.

—ANN LANDERS

Affirmations

I accept my God-given power over my world of effects.
Divine Love in and through me expresses as friends and
companions wherever I go.
                    —Dr. Delia Sellers

Speaking Skills

We can give of ourselves in many ways and public speaking is
number one on the list of things people fear most. It seems most
people would rather die than speak before a group of people.
Public speaking is an art form and a gift. It is an art form in that
you have to create the experience you want your audience to have
moment by moment. You will need mastery over the ability to
express your ideas and opinions in a logical, orderly manner. And
be able to think quickly, and speak to the issue when called upon,
at a moment's notice. A cost-effective simplistic training program
is a toastmistress or toastmaster group. For the club listing in your
locality, check the phone directory or contact your local chamber
of commerce. To overcome your fear of speaking before others,
tape record yourself speaking for one minute on a topic that
interest you, and that you love.

Speaking is made up of two ingredients a speaker and an
audience. Both are necessary for the production of the show. The
speaker must be comfortable with the audience and the audience
must be comfortable with the speaker. Gene Perret gives six
suggestions to help a speaker be at ease with an audience:

1. **Don't Be Afraid of the Audience.** "People are not afraid of
   the stage, they are afraid of the audience. An audience feels
   rejected when you are afraid of them." If you If you are good
   the audience will let you know it, and if you are bad they will
   let you know it. If the audience dislikes you, it means you must
   work more on your material, your presentation, or yourself.

2. **Respect Your Audience.** —"You are behind the microphone

to make your listeners feel good. You do that as simply as any good host would. You respect them and make them feel wanted and welcome.

3. **You Owe Your Audience Preparation.** —Top-notch performers know they have to be prepared each time they step onto a stage.

4. **Be Aware Of the Audience's Problem**—Can everyone see you. If not move around. Is the sound system weak? If so speak out loudly and enunciate. Have other speaker before you talked too long? If so be brief. The message you want he audience to get is, "no matter what the conditions, I'm still good."

5. **Be On Time**—The audience is giving you their valuable time so respect that. Be prepared to go when you agreed to go on.

· **Be Gracious**—Your performing time is not limited by your introduction and your closing sentence. You can't be a good speaker without a healthy respect and genuine fondness for each person you appear before.

According to Lillian Brown in her book, *Your Public Best*, she lists several qualities of the voice:
1. Resonance
2. Placement, whether it is on a low, middle, or high register
3. Pitch
4. Volume
5. Projection (using the diaphragmatic muscles to fill the lungs with air to push words out the mouth)
6. Timbre
7. Expression
8. Tone
9. Nasality (the nasal tone quality is harsh, unpleasant to the ear, and to be avoided when speaking publicly).

And she lists the characteristics of a good and bad voice. A good speaking voice is: Pleasant, Resonant, Relaxed, Well modulated,

Low pitched, Controlled, Warm, Melodic, Concerned, Eloquent, Confident, Authoritative, Agreeable, Colorful, Expressive, Natural, Rich, Full, audible, and Positive.

A bad Speaking voice is Nasal, Harsh or strident, Hoarse or raspy,, Tremulous, High pitched or shrill, Whiny, Breathy, Timid, Choppy, Too Loud, Too soft or inaudible, Ineffective, Pompous, Sarcastic in tone, Hesitant, Flat or monotonous, Tense, Weak, or Dull. I highly recommend her book or a similar one. I have taken voice lessons from two speaking coaches and I still found a wealth of information in her book. If you want to speak for a fee, and have someone pay you for your talent, I suggest you secure the services of a speaking coach you can work with comfortably. Your voice is an instrument. And the words you speak, can tear a person down or build them up. What are you willing to do to become better in your profession or career?

My Personal Commitment To Improve Are:

Write your answers and comments in your notebook

If You Can Imagine It, You Can Achieve It.
If You Can Dream It, You Can Become It.
—KRISTONE

Presentation Skills

This is a two-fold process. It is a good idea to attend one of the free wardrobe shows given by one of the local department stores. Call to ask when and if such event is being offered. If you are unable to attend a free session, it would be worth your money to have a color analysis done by a professional, to ascertain which colors best bring out your skin tone coloring. What is your body type frame, and the best style clothing to wear to emphasize or de-emphasize certain body proportions.

The other part of the process is to secure the services of a voice coach, or theatrical coach who has access to video feedback so that you can see and hear how you come across to others as you present yourself. Again in many toastmasters club, this is sometimes available for free, but the feedback may not be as detailed as you might like.

If finances are a consideration for you, you can tape record a message and play it back, then critique yourself. Also you can give a presentation standing in front of the mirror. Pay close attention to your body posture, i.e. the way you hold your head to one side, raise one shoulder, body rigidity and breathing pattern.

Ask several friends or two different neighbors to critique your presentation, and to give you objective feedback. Tell them you want the truth, even if it is unpleasant. You might write out a list of things you want them to check off, to make it easier for them in their critique of you. Some people have trouble saying unpleasant things--when asked for an opinion.

Use your enthusiasm to help you stand out and connect with others. Its benefits are many: Enthusiasm permits no room for anything derogatory. It automatically discards criticism and converts it to praise. Enthusiasm recognizes the value of everything. It is positive talk and positive action. Enthusiasm leaves no room for boredom. It is a method of diplomacy and persuasion. It is a way to get others to help themselves and help you. It establishes spirit and cooperation at little or no cost.

How to Develop Enthusiasm:
Have a desire to do something.
Find a happy side to every situation.
Turn your enthusiasm on even when you do not feel enthusiastic.
Pretend you are happy about some occasion or event
    if you do not have one.
Show interest in things and people. Develop many interests
    and see the bright side to each.
Make each new thing you do a challenge.
Step up your desire to achieve.
Widen your horizons, find new studies, new friends, new travel,
    discover new faces and friends to share the span of your
    personal view.

Find something to inspire you to start anew.
Do what you enjoy doing.
Avoid negative, complaining grumbling people.
Change the pace of your life with new friends acquaintances,
    new desire, a new vision, new drive and a new you.
Decide to become a vibrant, loving, caring person.
Think enthusiasm, act enthusiastic, and be enthusiastic.
Anything that you play act long enough will eventually
    become a reality.
Enthusiasm is a learned behavior, it has to be developed
    because it is generated inside the person.
To influence another person you will need to rev up
    your enthusiasm.

Affirmation
I see life as filled with unlimited opportunities and possibilities.

On Habits
*The beginning of a habit is like an invisible thread, every
time we repeat the act we strengthen the strand, add to it
another filament, until it becomes a great cable and binds
us irrevocably, thought and act.* —ORISON SWETT MARDEN

Chapter 3

Professional Skills Needed
For Business Success

*The greatest discovery of my generation is that human beings can
alter their lives by altering their attitude of mind.*
—WILLIAM JAMES

Selling Ability or Desire for Challenge
Are you ready for business success? To be successful in any
endeavor you must have sales ability. You must be able to sell the
greatest commodity in the world, yourself. You will need to be a
salesperson, and good sales people are not born, they are created.
The following are traits of top sales people: They have an above
average ability and motivation to sell.

3. They are self-starters
4. They do or act, rather than talk.
5. They enjoy selling.

They may be uncomfortable doing detailed duties, but they are
excellent at selling. To be a success in life, you will need to
become good at selling. All of life is about selling. And you are the
product you will be selling to the world. Learn to esteem yourself
daily, to be a better sales person. To help you in this area, our book
Self-Esteem, The Essence of You—The Milestones of Life is a good
tool to have.

We were born to create, to be productive in life. Have you
decided what you will do, or how you will make your livelihood?
According to E.V. Ingram in his book, *Wells Of Abundance,*
"Physical work is only a means of outward expression. It builds
muscles not character. It is the working of the mind back of the
muscle that builds skills." What he is saying is, it's the attitude you
take about your tasks in life that builds character, not just work

itself. And all growth involves change.

We come to a point in life, when we have to decide if we want to take the risk to move in a different direction, or if we are satisfied with maintaining our status quo of mediocrity, to remain secure in our self-constricted cocoon.

In his book, *Making It Happen*, by Charles Paul Conn, quotes the following:

> "We must never be ashamed of wanting more. We must never be embarrassed by our hunger. We must never believe that to strive for a better world, or a better life, is somehow an act of disloyalty to the old one. We must always be willing to be hungry-hungry to sing a better song, write a better letter, bowl a higher score, make a bigger profit, set a better example, give more support to the causes and people and organizations we believe in. For when we are no longer hungry for that , we lose something precious. When we quit stretching, we quit growing; we quit living."

If you are a Christian, do not feel it is unchristian to want more in life or better your circumstances and conditions. When you want more good in life, you will need to be a bigger and better person to reach your goals. For we accomplish our goals by working through others.

Also you will need a burning desire to achieve, that will inspire you to want to move up the success ladder. If you have not given this much thought, take time now to do so. Decide what challenge or challenges you would like to overcome. Give yourself a time frame. You need a compelling reason or reasons to inspire you onward with your career. Write out your goals. Keep them in view, so that you can see them often. What is your challenge? Is it to move to a better neighborhood? Get new braces for your child's teeth? Install a swimming pool or a Jacuzzi in your back yard? Get a weekly pedicure, manicure, and facial? Make $50,000 a year? Become the first female corporate executive in your firm? You need a desire for challenge. Decide what challenge or challenges you would like to overcome, and when you plan to accomplish the goal and remember to set realistic goals. You may need to enroll in

Adult Education classes to sharpen your skills, or you may need to attend Junior College or a university to acquire the necessary skills for the job you desire. Maybe you will be the first person in your family to graduate from college.

Do you have a strong enough challenge that will propel you, to move up the success ladder? Sales ability and selling are two different activities. Selling is often interpreted as an effort to overcome the opposition. When you take this approach, people are seen as your enemy rather than your friend or allay.

A good example of this concept is summarized by Cicero in his writings on "The Six Mistakes Of Man:

1. *The delusion that personal gain is made by crushing others.*
2. *The tendency to worry about things that cannot be changed or corrected.*
3. *Insisting that a thing is impossible because we cannot accomplish it.*
4. *Refusing to set aside trivial preferences.*
5. *Neglecting development and refinement of the mind, and not acquiring the habit of reading and studying.*
· *Attempting to compel others to believe and live as we do.*
—CICERO, ROMAN STATESMAN AND PHILOSOPHER, 106 BC

Opportunism. To succeed in the Business world you will need to be an opportunistic entrepreneur. Each day you live, you tread on uncharted terrain. Keep a keen eye. Be forever looking out for new opportunities; when you see one, seize it. It may not come back again. Keep an open mind. Be kind, cordial and considerate to all people regardless of the sex, race or creed. The hand you help today, may be the one to lift you after a devastating loss in your career. Pause often to count your gains and your losses. Whatever you do, do it with style and class. Do it with gusto, heart, vim and vigor. If you are a leader act like a leader. Remember, all good leaders know how to follow when necessary.

How To Get What You Want In Life

You Can Have Anything You Want__
If You Want It Badly Enough.
You Can Be Anything You Want To Be,
Have, Anything You Set Out To Accomplish__
If You Will Hold To That Desire
With Singleness Of Purpose.
—ROBERT COLLIER

Take A Chance

Even a turtle gets nowhere until he sticks his neck out.
On the plains of Hesitation, Bleach the bones of unnumbered
thousands, who at the dawn of victory,
sat down to wait—and waiting, died.

Success is for those energetic enough to work for it.
Hopeful enough to look for it, Patient enough to wait for it,
Brave enough to seize it, and strong enough to hold it
—ANON

The Power of Change

All of life is about change, change is good for us yet we resist and fight it vehemently. Change creates tension, and tension is uncomfortable. Since we are creatures of comfort, we dislike change because we feel tense, nervous, and uncomfortable.

Most people resist change because they feel threatened. They fear they may lose something which they value. Because the new idea or process does not fit within the boundaries of their current paradigms, so they resist or seek to prove the new idea is wrong, inappropriate or unnecessary.

A paradigm is the set of rules or criteria you use to judge whether something is correct or appropriate. A paradigm is a filter of perception; it is the frame you put around a concept in order to understand it and make it fit with your understanding of the world in which you live. We

53

all use paradigms to organize our perceptions. When we do a double take because we have observed or experienced something odd, when we argue intensely against a new idea, it is because our paradigms have been challenged. Think about the values, habits, processes and rules which direct your activities.

These are your paradigms.

Write your answers and comments in your notebook

1. What paradigms do you want to keep?
2. Which do you want to reject?
3. What paradigms are changing or shifting for you?
4. What new paradigms do you predict for your company, or self?
5. What today seems impossible, but if it could be done would radically change the way you live, or do business?

Because change is such an unpleasant feeling, you will only change:

1. when you are ready and willing, when you see a need, when you are discontent, when you can benefit by being different
2. When you see a need and know how—You must change your facts, ideas, attitudes, beliefs, and emotions, change requires your skill, patience, and understanding.
3. You change when you are mentally and/or physically involved — You must involve and alter your intellect and emotions, you must actively participate in the change process, and construct new habit patterns.
4. You change when you see a personal gain—So sell the benefits to yourself so you can accept the change, you must cooperate with the proposed change that meets your goals and objectives.

Some factors that inhibit change are:
*   Fear of loss,
*   Status quo inertia,
*   Future uncertainty,
*   Lack of involvement,

- When you don't see the need,
- It upsets the power balance,
- Change,
- Equal criticism,
- The change agent is incompetent,
- Misunderstandings,
- There is a history of antagonism,
- A violation of values,
- Bad timing,
- Lack of organizational identity,
- Resistance/power from resistant factions, or
- Implementing the change would disrupt important relationships.

When Asking For A Behavioral Change
<u>Describe</u>
- Describe the other person's behavior objectively.
- Use concrete terms.
- Describe a specified time, place, and frequency of action.
- Describe the action, not the "motive."

<u>Express</u>
- Express your feelings.
- Express your feelings calmly.
- State feelings in a positive manner related to goal.
- Direct yourself to the specific offensive behavior, not the person.

<u>Empathize</u>
- Show some understanding of the other persons' position.
- Be honest, not sarcastic

<u>Specify</u>
- Ask explicitly for a change in behavior.
- Request a small change.

- Request only one or two changes at one time.
- Specify the actions you want to see stopped, and those you want to see performed.
- Take account of whether your person can meet your request without suffering huge loss.
- Specify what behavior you are willing to change to get the agreed change in behavior.

Consequences
- Make the consequences explicit.
- Give a positive reward for change in the desired direction.
- Select something that is desirable and reinforcing for the other person.
- Select a reward that is big enough to maintain the behavioral change.
- Select a punishment of magnitude that "fits the crime" of refusing to change behavior.
- Select a punishment that you are willing to carry out.

What change do you fear in your life at this time? Does the change involve your career, finances, relationships, business associations or affiliations? The changes we fear the most seem to be associated with our money making ability or work activities. Are you afraid of being fired, or relocated in your present work?

I Am Thought, Thinking My Form,
Feelings And Conditions. —ANON

Do not be fearful if you are fired. Being fired may be the best thing that could happen to your career. You may have reached a plateau in your former job. A variety of experiences can be critical to the advancement of your career. The path to the top of the corporate ladder is not always straight. You may need to move horizontally or diagonally to advance your career. Or move to another job if it is to your advantage.

If you can get free training in high technology or computer

science, take it. You may have to start on a lower entry pay level, but the ability to advance within the corporation may be excellent. Be willing to take a risk. Comfort is not always growth. You may be very comfortable in your present job environment, but how far will you have advanced in ten years? Will you be making the $100,000 you had set out to make within ten years? (If that is your goal) Always maintain a competitive edge for yourself. This produces stress and stress does not feel good. Even though it may be good for you. All stress is not bad. Eustress is a form of good stress. Stress is a behavioral outlet of unresolved inner personal or interpersonal issues. You will need to have clarity, and a clear sense of direction for your life before the dynamic tension of stress subsides.

Indicators of Stress

Physical
Fatigue
Nausea
Muscle Tremors
Headaches
Visual Difficulties
Heightened/Lowered Alertness
Teeth Grinding
Weakness

Cognitive
Blaming someone
Confusion
Poor Attention
Poor Decisions
Creativity Loss
Memory Problems
Poor Concentration
Poor Problem Solving

Emotional
Anxiety
Guilt
Grief
Denial
Fear
Uncertainty
Depression
Overwhelmed
Suspiciousness

Behavioral
Withdrawal
Emotional Outbursts
Inability to Relax or Sleep Well
Change In Usual Communication
Loss or Increase of Appetite
Increase of Alcohol or Drugs
Intense Anger Feeling
Acting like A Victim
Fear

To successfully overcome stress, you need to be aware of eight underlying negative emotions. They are anger, anxiety, guilt, distrust, envy, greed, selfishness and sorrow. If you are willing to commit to change these negative emotions to positive, you will have more energy and feel more alive.

My Personal Commitment To Change Is:

Write about your commitment to change in your notebook

Making Changes

Write your answers and comments in your notebook

- Identify a challenge confronting you
- Describe the future state. What will the situation be like when the change has been implemented?
- Describe the present state. What is happening in the situation now?
- What action steps are needed to implement the change?
- What factors are helping the change?
- What factors are hindering the change?
- Who will the change impact?

Attitude
1. It is our attitude at the beginning of a task which, more than anything else, will affect its successful outcome.
2. It is our attitude towards life which will determine life's attitude towards us.
3. We are interdependent. It is impossible to succeed without others; and it is our attitude toward others which will determine their attitude towards us.
4. The higher you go in any organization of value, you will find, the better will be the attitude.
5. Before a person can achieve the kind of life they want, they must become that kind of individual — they must Think, Act, Talk, Walk, and Conduct themselves in all of their affairs, as

58

would the person they wish to become.

6. Your mind can only hold only one thought at a time. Since there's nothing to be gained by holding negative thoughts, hold successful positive thoughts.
7. The deepest craving of human beings is to be needed, to feel important, to be appreciated. Give it to them and they'll return it to you.
8. Part of a good attitude is to look for the best in new ideas---- and look for good ideas everywhere.
9. Don't talk about your health unless it's good — unless you're talking to your doctor.
10. Don't waste your time broadcasting personal problems. It won't help you and it cannot help others.
11. Radiate the attitude of well-being, of confidence, of a person who shows where he's going. You'll find good things will start happening right away.
12. Lastly for the next thirty days, treat everyone with whom you come in contact as the most important person on earth. If you can do this for thirty days, you'll do it for the rest of your life. Start today.

Negotiation Skills, The Power to Influence,
Desire for competition. You will need a strong, healthy desire for competition to move up the corporate ladder. There may be times when the odds are against you. However, if you have a strong drive to achieve, you can withstand the opposition. Be willing to take a risk to advance your career. Plan before hand to have a contingency plan in case things do not turn out as you had planned. Be willing to compromise or negotiate if necessary. Try to gauge in advance just how far you can go before you reach a point of no return. Know when to push and when to pull. Also know when to quit. Don't be discouraged if you risk and lose. Nothing ventured, nothing gained.
Desire for Power. To move up the business, success ladder you will need to have a healthy desire for power. Power is the ability to

get people to do what you want them to, and the ability to avoid being forced to do what you don't want to do. Some key guidelines to know about power are:

1. **Build relationships**. Gratitude and obligation can give you power leverage. Make sure the people working under you have a positive impression of you. They are more likely to trust you and want to do as you suggest.

2. **Your power base** increases as the number of people dependent on you increases.

3. **Establish credibility**. Stand behind what you say and do.

4. **Become an expert**. Develop a reputation as an expert, this way others will come to rely on you and defer to your judgment.

5. **Data control.** Control as much as possible the flow of information. To have privileged information that others desire can increase your power base immensely.

6. **Control.** What resources are you able to control? The key ones are money, employees, equipment.

7. **Be interested in other people**. Know how people feel about important issues; seek to win their respect.

8. **Know the sources of Power**. Observe and listen in to the grapevine. Who are the movers in the organization? Who is quoted most often? Pay attention to these tidbits of information.

9. **Be willing to take a risk.** Be willing to risk the power you have to obtain more.

10. **Avoid losing power**. Sidestep activities and projects that could have an adverse effect on the power you have.

11. **Be ethical**. Don't lie, cheat, or break your promises

12. **Know how can you impact the lives of others**. If you are in charge of memos, meetings, agendas or schedules, others will need your approval, which places you in a position of power too.

13. **Be aware of how your actions are viewed by others.**
    Are you seen as supporting others, or do you have a
    label as a self-serving individual?
14. **Employees.** The greater your responsibilities, the more
    you will need to rely on the cooperation and help of
    others. Unless the people working under you are loyal
    to you, they may not follow your orders. Seek to
    establish some trusting and bonding alliances of a few
    key people to leverage your power base? It helps to
    know whether you are inner (introvert) or outer
    (extrovert) directed.

Write your responses in your notebook

1. I am an... Introvert/Extrovert
2. I get angry.. Easily/Rarely
3. I stick with problems............................ Yes/No
4. I go out of my way to get attention....... Yes/No
5. I prefer.. Leading/Following
6. I need friends .... Yes/No
7. When threatened, I.............................. Attack/Retreat
8. I feel guilty .... Often/Seldom
9. I need social approval .... Yes/No
10. I wait for things to happen.................. True/False
11. I am .... Cautious/Impulsive
12. I like close attachments to people........ True/False
13. To control my emotions is................... Easy/Difficult
14. I enjoy new fads/fashions.................... True/False
15. Confronting others is........................... Difficult/Easy
16. I get bored easily................................ True/False
17. I enjoy doing small things for people... True/False
18. I find competition................................ Enjoyable/Distasteful
19. I will make a great contribution in life. True/False

The Optimist Creed

Promise Yourself To: Be so strong that nothing can disturb your peace of mind.

Talk health, happiness and prosperity to every person you meet. To make all your friends feel that there is something in them.

To look at the sunny side of everything and make your optimism come true.

To think only of the best, to work for only the best—and to expect only the best.

To be just as enthusiastic about the success of others, as you are about your own.

To forget mistakes of the past and press on to the greatest achievements of the future.

To wear a cheerful countenance at all times and give every living creature you meet a smile.

To give so much time to the improvement of yourself that you have no time to criticize others.

To be too large for worry, too noble for anger, too strong for fear, and too happy to permit the presence of trouble...

—OPTIMIST INTERNATIONAL

Remember, power is about forming and maintaining dependent and interdependent relationships with persons under your leadership. It can be good or bad, constructive or destructive. The choice is yours.

Beliefs About Conflict I believe that conflict...

Write your beliefs in your notebook

Unresolved inner personal conflict or interpersonal conflict will manifest as stress. Stress is a behavioral outlet of unresolved inner personal or interpersonal issues. By changing your life style behavior patterns. Most of us recognize the fact that we have stress in our life. What we often fail to recognize or to act upon is the various ways that we can manage our own stress level. It seems that it is easier to blame others for it and to remain the way we are.

Changing behaviors and attitudes appear to cause us too much discomfort. Therefore it is easier to remain in a stress overload condition. The following will give you hints and skills in how to manage and survive stress.

1. In life there are some things over which we have no control. Try to identify that these things are in your life.
2. Do not try to change the perceptions or feelings of others. You are not in control of anyone else's thoughts or feelings. You can influence, request, demand, and attempt other method's of control, but people do what they want to do; they feel what they want to feel and they think what they want to think.
3. Many times we become stressful over that which we know nothing about. Find out.
4. Avoid too many changes in too short a time.
5. Beware of "should". "You should do everything well." What will happen if you do not do everything well?
6. Be willing to be less than perfect. You don't have to get to the top or be loved by everyone that meets you.
7. Practice accepting what you cannot change.
8. Take one step at a time; pace yourself.
9. Be with people that respect you, accept you, listen to you, touch you, validate you and support you. There is no reason to tolerate constant abuse, criticism, withdrawal, or indifference. Be around people who are good for you.
10. Does your life reflect your needs or do you respond only to demands of others?
11. Take care of your body because it is the only one that you have. Get plenty of sleep and rest. Cut down on sugar, alcohol, drugs, coffee, and tobacco. Exercise daily. Learn relaxation techniques. Find some time to be alone and peaceful.
12. Try to block interruptions. Think ahead of responses to use when you are busy and do not want to break your train of thought.
13. Plan ahead to reduce probability of surprise.

14. Communicate openly and honestly with those in your life using effective communication and active listening skills.

Conversational Strategies
Here are some suggestions for making conversation easier and less frustrating:

1. The person speaking will be better understood if they:
   · Make sure the listener knows the topic being discussed.
   · Speak slowly, clearly and with a natural flow
     (avoid exaggerating speech sounds).
   · Ask the listener to watch their face.
   · Get reasonably close to the listener.
   · Rephrase (use other words) rather than repeating if the
     listener can't understand.
   · Avoid speaking in noisy places.
   · When possible, use a gesture to <u>show</u> what they mean.
   · Write or spell the message aloud if saying it won't work.
   · Be patient, the listener is probably doing their
     best to understand.

2. The person listening will understand better if they:
   · Make sure they know the speaker's topic
   · May attention to the speaker's face
   · Get reasonably close to the speaker
   · Ask for a repeat or rephrase (do not pretend to understand
     or "fake it"
   · Ask the speaker to spell or write the message if it is
     just not clear
   • Be patient, the speaker is probably doing their best
     to speak clearly.

On Disputes

How many a dispute could have been deflated into a single paragraph if the disputants had dared to define their terms?
—ARISTOTLE

Why We Don't Assert Ourselves

Write your answers and comments in your notebook

What do you fear about asserting yourself?

What are some benefits of asserting yourself?

Success Over Stress Lifestyle Assessment

Write your responses in your notebook

Rate Yourself On A Scale of 1-4
  Never = 4
  Occasionally = 3
  Often = 2
  Always = 1

1. ...I spend time alone
2. ...I express my true feelings and can be myself
3. ...I am relaxed when waiting in lines, in traffic, or for someone.
4. ...I spend quality time with my family or friends.
5. ...I am satisfied with my physical appearance.
6. ...I like my job
7. ...I am in control of my life.
8. ...I feel problems can be potential opportunities.
9. ...I am free of worries and anxieties.
10. ...I am free of time pressure.
11. ...I feel love and support from family and friends.

12. ...I expect good things to happen to me.
13. ...I know when to say no.
14. ...I find time to be of service to others.
15. ...I am free of work-related thoughts when not working.
16. ...I accept life changes easily.
17. ...I eat foods which are good for me.
18. ...I exercise regularly.
19. ...I laugh and have fun.
20. ...I feel rested upon awakening.
21. ...I complete tasks and follow through on commitments
     and agreements.
22. ...I am free from health-related worries.
23. ...I accept other exactly the way they are.
24. ...Others view me as easy going.
25. ...I feel good to be alive.
26. ...I find time to appreciate nature.
27. ...I establish priorities for my time.
28. ...I find time for hobbies.
29. ...I express my creativity and utilize my potential.
30. ...My life is in balance.

Yes You Can!

Think win-win, because you'll not win in the long run if the
     other person walks away humiliated. You'll pay some
     where down the line.

Focus on issues, not personalities, and remain calm. Name-
     calling and hurling accusations make a bad situation worse.
     The more upset you get, the less sense you make and less
     credibility you have.

Listen to others' assertions before making yours. Once they've
     spoken their piece, they will be better listeners, and you
     will be armed with information when it's your turn to
     speak. You may even hear some valid points.

Ask lots of questions to learn *why* others believe what they are
     saying is true.

Limit your description of situations to what can be observed, as opposed to what you suspect or surmise. Deal in fact, not innuendo. When you assert your view, state *why* you believe your belief.

Monitor and control your non-verbal communication. Don't tense up, point finger, scowl, or get in the person's face. Maintain eye contact without glaring.

Fix the future, rather than rehash the past. Think long-term. Ask, "What will it take to keep this from happening again?

Keep the focus on your comparative needs, not your opposing *positions*. Engage with the other person in a search for creative ways to meet both sets of needs and reach common ground.

—EXCERPTED FROM *Yes, You Can!* BY SAM DEEP AND LYLE SUSSMAN, ADDISON-WESLEY PUBLISHING CO.

The Power Of Imaging Our Possibilities

Go confidently in the direction of your dreams.
Live the life you have imagined.
—HENRY DAVID THOREAU

Leadership Skills

The ability to delegate is a skill worth developing in yourself. As you move up the corporate ladder and assume more responsibilities, you will need the assistance of others to maximize your time, effort and resources.

Foremost of all, decide what tasks you will delegate and which you will do yourself. Once you delegate, let the individuals know up front that you may need to make corrections as you go along and that you will need input from them; also tell that you will need input from them. In addition, you will have periodic reviews to gauge the success of the project. This way they will be expecting to be accountable to you for their work activities. If you lay out the ground rules before hand, they are less likely to view you as meddling when you inquire about their activities later. You might want to agree on an acceptable review conference. If the project before you has a time deadline, you may need to have a weekly or monthly review.

Here are some points you want to keep in mind as you decide what to delegate to whom:

1. **The Buck Stops With You.** You will be held accountable whether the project fails or succeed. You will lose the loyalty of your subordinates if they are blamed for the failure. Also your superiors will not respect you if you place the blame on your subordinates. Just admit that the situation did not turn out as you expected.

2. **Know What To Delegate.** If you have been asked to handle the task, don't delegate it. They want your expertise. Even though the task may be very simple. Someone respects your abilities. Be glad.

3. **Be Selective.** Delegate the right task to the right person. Try to match the skills of the task to the person. You will be less likely to hear complaints and you will be pleased to know that the job is in competent hands.

4. **Be Explicit.** Make certain your delegates understand what they are to do. Have well defined goals. Ask for clarification and feedback. If they can state back to you the overall concept of what you said you have obtained your objective.

5. **Responsibility.** Try to foster a sense of responsibility in your delegates. Let them know you are counting on them to do well.

6. **Authority.** Define the limits of authority they will have. Let them know that the authority may be shared between you and them. However, if possible assign them total responsibility for minor job tasks. Let them know that they need to check with you if ever they are doubtful about overstepping their boundaries.

7. **Decision-Making.** Plan on making the big decisions yourself and let them analyze, advise and recommend.
8. **Independent Action.** Encourage independence. Allow your delegates to act, without checking with you before their every move. This will help them feel that you have confidence in them. Also it will help them to feel more competent in what they are doing. Focus more on "what" they do, rather than "how" they carry out your instructions.
9. **Expect Excellence.** Set the example, expect high standards of workmanship from both yourself and those working under you. Let them know in advance that you want quality workmanship. Think of ways you can reinforce this behavior, through some form of positive reinforcement.
10. **Rewards.** People will not work for long without some form of reward. Be supportive. Try to operate more as a team leader. Encourage and coach rather than dictate. Encourage them to succeed. Let them and others above you, know when they have done a good job. This will bolster their morale, and motivate them to work harder to be a good team member.

    Know when things have run off-track. Make necessary corrections when needed. If negative feedback is needed use the sandwich approach. State two positive factors, give the negative corrective feedback, then end with a positive statement. Let them know they are still an important part of the team. Take every opportunity to build up their morale and they will in turn do the same for you.
11. **Build Trust and Respect.** Strive mutual trust and respect from those working under your leadership. Take the necessary time to build an atmosphere of trust, respect, cooperation and open communication. This may take some time, but the long-term benefits are worth it to you.

If this is your first time having subordinates work under you, be understanding. Don't place the whole workload on them at once. Share some of the workload. It will help them to see you as a caring superior. It will make them work even harder to support you and your goals. The ability to delegate is an art and will take time and practice. Be a good team manager. Working as a team manager allows you to demonstrate independent leadership.

12. **Independence.** To move up the corporate ladder you will need to show that you are a leader. Leaders do not need group approval or reinforcement to bolster their self-esteem. They tend to view groups as a means of sharing ideas, information and problem solving.

All corporate executives have to be willing to take risks to advance their careers. Risk taking means to act, in hope, the outcome is favorable. If you have a fear of failure or are uncertain, you may want to be more pragmatic and avoid taking big risks. Confront your fears and act when it is wise. Rely on your intuition to guide you.

Always have a clear idea of how much power and authority you have. Know your limitations. Use wisdom and good judgment. There will be times when you should not act. Rely on your intuitions to guide you.

Treatment For Self Control

My peace is from within, and is not disturbed by anything outside of me. I am in control of my thoughts, my feelings and my reactions. I develop a habit of mindfulness, whereby I remember to be aware of myself when I am provoked, and I consciously refrain from over-reacting. I have a right to my opinion, but I do not have the right to inflict anger upon anyone. And I no longer wish to inflict it on myself! I intend to heal myself of this problem, and I accept my healing now. —IDA GREENE

Everything we think, say or do has a consequence in our life. What we love, desire, fear or hate, we bring to us in the same communicative pattern. Effective communication identifies, and describes the action you desire, and ignores the motive of what the other person is saying. It also helps you to control fear and anxiety.

Cohen, Fink, Gadon, and Willits in their book, *Effective Behavior In Organizations*, gives guidelines to ensure effective communication:

1. Choose Your Words-talk in words that are likely to have meaning and clarity to the other person, anticipate different ways your message could be interpreted, allow yourself to be spontaneous and open.
2. Attend To Nonverbal Messages-Pay attention to tone of voice, facial expressions, body posture, hesitations; what do they communicate, in addition to the message in the words? Are you congruent? Does your tone of voice fit your words and reflect your inner feeling?
3. Timing and Situation-Don't raise "heavy issues" when the other person is preoccupied or there isn't time to deal with them properly. Consider the setting when you raise a topic for discussion. Ignore small points you may differ with and focus on the main theme. Deal with issues and tensions early; handle problem while they are small.
4. Testing For Understanding-Invite the other person to restate what you've said in his/her own words and test whether you've been clear.
5. Preserve the Relationship-Give the other person an opportunity to be heard, be careful you aren't so busy preparing your response that you don't pay full attention. Don't interrupt. Acknowledge that which is of worth in what someone is saying, even if you disagree with the basic message.

Some Thoughts On Leadership

Good Leaders *are forward thinking.*

Good Leaders *are always one step ahead of the team.*

Good Leaders *are thoroughly knowledgeable about all big-picture goals and use this perspective to evaluate the worth of each activity.*

Good Leaders *pursue lives of balance, not of devotion to a single cause. The most successful leaders are well rounded. They are aware of events in the world around them and pursue outside interests.*

Good Leaders *continually reinforce the benefits of striving for a particular mission.*

Good Leaders *remind the team members of the goal when the team veers off track.*

Good Leaders *care about the details, and they account for them by delegating the most important ones to reliable team members.*

Good Leaders *realize the inter-dependency of his team with other teams, that the success of his operation is often linked to the success of other organizations.*

Good Leaders *wouldn't ask their team members to do anything they wouldn't also be prepared to do.*

Good Leaders *are accessible to all members of the team, the constituency they represent, and others who inquire about the process, the direction and mission of the operation, or the purpose of a change.*

Good Leaders *are not afraid to ask for help. Occasionally, people in leadership positions won't ask for help because they think it will make them look bad or that they have an inability to handle a task. Quite simply, this is a fallacy.*

Good Leaders *remember where they come from and have learned from their experiences. They soak up knowledge from every occurrence, professional and personal.*

Good Leaders *believe that motivation is knowing what truly excites you, and doing it; and that discipline is knowing what it is that you should do, not wanting to do it, but doing it anyway.* —K. MILLHONE

All-powerful leaders possess charisma, do you have it or do you need to improve in this area?
Write in your notebook the ones you have.

The Seven Characteristics of Charisma

- Self-confidence
- Warmth
- Friendliness
- Openness
- Approachability
- Sensitivity
- Vulnerability

Learning Channels Inventory

Write in your notebook four to six statements that tell how you prefer to learn.

When learning, I prefer to learn by:

a. Working with real things
b. Talking to myself while reading a book or questions on a test
c. Reading material about what I'm learning
d. Sketching or doodling while I'm learning
e. Hearing things explained first
f. Watching a filmstrip or film
g. Working with materials related to what is being learned
h. Listening to tapes, the radio or recordings
i. Watching someone illustrate or demonstrate the information
j. Performing through simulations, games or role-plays
k. Listening to experts describe and explain information.
l. Looking at charts, maps, graphs or pictures

When studying something to remember it, I prefer to:

Write your preferences in order of 1, 2, 3 in your notebook

- Say it to myself
- Write it
- Read it

When I am learning something new and want to understand it, I prefer to:

Write your preferences in order of 1, 2, 3 in your notebook

- read about it
- play a game to learn it
- listen to a teacher or expert explain it

Chapter 4

You Can't Have Business
Success Without These

The Ability To Balance Empathy And Objectivity.
Our future is what we make it. Nothing in the world stands still.
Change is normal, it is the one thing constant in life. Nothing
grows that does not change. Therefore we must keep producing
effort that gives positive results. The business world does not pay
for effort. It pays for results, and results comes from your knowing
who you are, what you want, where you are going and how you
plan to get there.

So take a look at your life and do some deep soul searching.
Think about your past, both positive and negative areas. Look at
how you have been treated and how you have treated others —
family members, friends, strangers, your property, the property of
others, and your pets if you had any. Did you act your best? Were
you as kind as you could have been? Were you sensitive to the
needs of others, or was your focus mostly on yourself?

Take a day for introspection and self-evaluation. Are you
pleased with your efforts today?

Your attitude about what happens to you is critical, for it will
be either positive or negative. Remember your attitude determines
your altitude. Your attitude is an inner personal communication to
the self about your:
1. Goals, desires, wishes, doubts, fears, or anxieties.
2. Thoughts
3. Emotions

Your communication is the use of words signals, gestures,
body language or any expressive behavior you show that is
interpreted by another person, has meaning for/to them that, they
understand or recognize from past associations.

Everything we think, say or do has a consequence in life. What we love, desire, fear or hate, we bring to us in the same communicative pattern. Effective communication identifies, and describes the action you desire, and ignores the motive of what the other person says.

Good communication helps you to control fear and anxiety. You do this by being in control of your mouth movement, jaw, and swallowing reflex. This can help you gain control over your emotions by requesting small changes in your behavior. It requires you to specify what behavior you are willing to change to get agreement with others or get what you want. It demands you be cooperative, because it shows others that you want to compromise. To be successful in your communication with others, you need to be tolerant of your and their imperfections and to express your feelings in a calm manner. It is wise to access all situations before you act.

Listening is the key to open, two-way communication. And responding with empathy shows that you understand the other person's feelings. When you listen, while responding with empathy you have caring, empathic, open communication.

It is important to let others know that you heard and understood both the content of what was said and the feelings expressed to you. When you get your feelings out in the open, it helps to focus on the topic before you. An effective empathic response describes the feelings expressed and sums up what the person said to convey the feeling. To respond with empathy does not mean you agree with what the other person is saying. An empathic response allows the other person to hear what you are saying, and you to receive information without extraneous distractions. When you react defensively you lose objectivity because you are unable to hear the intended message.

Dr. Delia Sellers says the six steps to become a better listener form a ladder:

L: Look at the person speaking to you.

A: Ask questions.

D: Don't interrupt.

D: Don't change the subject

E: Empathize (sense what others feel).

R: Respond verbally and non-verbally.

How To Command Attention
The Fine Art of Listening

Let the other person take center stage first. Once they have spoken their piece, they will be better listeners, and you will be armed with information when it's your turn to speak. You may even hear some valid points.

Ask lots of questions to learn *why* others believe what they are saying is true.

Limit your description of situations to what can be observed, as opposed to what you suspect or surmise. Deal in fact, not innuendo. When you assert your view, state *why* you believe your belief.

Monitor and control your non-verbal communication. Don't tense up, point finger, scowl, or get in the person's face. Maintain eye contact without glaring.

Fix the future, rather than rehash the past. Think long-term. Ask, "What will it take to keep this from happening again?

Keep the focus on your comparative needs, not your opposing *positions*. Engage with the other person in a search for creative ways to meet both sets of needs and reach common ground.

—EXCERPTED FROM *Yes, You Can!* BY SAM DEEP AND LYLE SUSSMAN, ADDISON-WESLEY PUBLISHING CO.

The Power Of Imaging Our Possibilities
Go confidently in the direction of your dreams.
Live the life you have imagined.
—HENRY DAVID THOREAU

As an executive, you want to take care that your objectivity is not hampered by your feelings, for you may need to play many roles. You want the ability to move in and out of a role quickly and gracefully. So you can be empathetic to the needs of others and maintain objectivity. The key is detachment. View yourself as a Judge who is giving an impartial decision, this way you can maintain a healthy balance between empathy and objectivity. Know your limitations. Be honest with your self. There are times when you may need to sidestep a situation because your objectivity is clouded by personal experiences. Know when to let go and move on. An example of this is an observation made by Sidney Harris, from an article he condensed from the Chicago Daily News — Do You Act-or React?

> I walked with a friend, a Quaker, to the newsstand the other night, and he bought a paper, thanking the newsboy politely. The newsboy didn't even acknowledge it."
>
> "A sullen fellow, isn't he?" I commented.
>
> "Oh, he's that way every night," shrugged my friend.
>
> "Then why do you continue to be so polite to him?"
>
> "Why not?" inquired my friend. "Why should I let him decide how I'm going to act? "As I thought about this incident later, it occurred to me that the important word was "act." My friend acts toward people; most of us react toward them. He has a sense of inner balance which is lacking in most of us; he knows who he is, what he stands for, how he should behave. He refuses to return incivility for incivility, because then he would no longer be in command of his conduct.

My Present Wishes/Hopes/Future Possibilities Are:

Write your answers and comments in your notebook

One Day At A Time

Do not look back and grieve over the past, for it is gone;
and do not be troubled about the future, for it has yet to come.

Live in the present, and make it so beautiful that it will be worth remembering.
                    —IDA SCOTT TAYLOR

People who succeed differ greatly from those who fail. What we believe to be true, becomes so.

What Are Some Of Your Unfulfilled Past Expectations Dreams or Fantasies

Write your answers and comments in your notebook

"I Can C.O.P.E"

Use the expression "I can C.O.P.E". as guide to improve the quality of your life. Include these concepts to control your response to adverse conditions, and weigh your options before you act:

1. Recognize and deal with your stressors one at a time.
2. Value all progress, however small or slight.
3. Remember, coping is a skill and requires daily attention for its full development.
4. Open up, by freely discussing your frustrations with close friends.
5. Build a social support system to buffer adversity.
6. Keep good communications, be open and candid.
7. Pace yourself by improving your planning and organization skills.
8. Remember, the goal is to end your day in the best possible physical and mental condition.
9. Put your mornings together to avoid rushing.
10. Prioritize your objectives for the day and allow flexibility.
11. Exercise and relax by improving your physical fitness and adding quiet time to your daily living.
12. Sustain your exercise for 30 minutes and repeat your program 3 to 4 times a week.

Relax by following these steps:

1. Sit comfortably with your eyes closed in a quiet location.
2. Slowly repeat a peaceful word or phrase over and over to yourself in your mind.
3. Take complete but comfortable breaths, inhaling through the nose and exhaling through the mouth.
4. Avoid distracting thoughts by keeping a passive mental attitude.

Prosperity Affirmations

I am prosperous. I never entertain thoughts of poverty or lack.

I am supplied from the Infinite Source with all that I need, with plenty to spare.

Right ideas come to me when I need them. I make right decisions at the right time.

I am never alone. I have a Silent Partner who works with me in everything I do. He is within me, working with me every moment of the day.

I have no regrets for the past, no fear for this moment nor any anxiety for the future. I am protected by an Infinite Power; I am guided by a Divine Intelligence; and I am sustained by It.

All is well and I am thankful. —JACK ADDINGTON

How to Transform The Invisible Into the Visible

The good that comes from your business is within you, and it flows from inside you to those persons who will purchase your goods. All businesses provide services, so our good (money) flows out from us to return to us multiplied. Our good is embodied within us. Therefore we must seek ways to express it, share it, and release it. We cannot get supply. Our supply is within us, in the form of the ideas, and services we provide.

What you get in life always equal your perception, expectation of what you will get. Your perceptions are formed by your thoughts, words, and feelings. Reverend Delia Sellers states, "they are the developments of your mind, which are symbolized by the words/language you speak. We get, manifest what ever we verbalize. What ever you speak about, you get more of. Your usual way of being in life is a pattern, based in language. The language determines the outcome. So the place to look for abundance is in your spoken word. The words you use, and speak, say, what is so for you. You cannot have whatever you cannot say and claim. If you cannot see what is fixed-in-your-mind, you remain with it, though unknowingly and cannot manifest it. Possibilities exist through possibility thinking. The possibilities you perceive depend on the habits of your perception; all limitations are only positions of perception.

Since our supply is within us, we must create an avenue for it to pour forth from us to those persons who are in need of our gifts, talents, or services. The two tools we can use to start the flow for our good is love and gratitude. Gratitude is powerful, because you share and give without a desire for a return.

Remember, you do not get money from God. God is the avenue of expression through which the substance of money flows to you as creative ideas. Your creative ideas come from Divine intuition and inspiration.

> *Affirm, daily "my good is never taken away from me, because I am dealing with an Infinite supply. Loss is out of my consciousness. What is mine by Divine Right I cannot lose, I open the door to the opportunities that awaits me today".* —DR. FRANK RICHELIEU

Most people do not realize their dreams or desired goals because they do not understand the principles of manifestation. David Spangler, in his book, **The Laws of Manifestation**, states "manifestation is the process of translating energy from one level to another. The movement of an idea within a person's consciousness from a vague, ambiguous state to one of clarity and understanding is a process of manifestation. Also, it can be translation, a means of elevating and uplifting, of raising the physical into the spiritual. One can translate an emotional or physical experience into wisdom and spiritual insight, or transfer energy from a lower to a higher level of awareness."

David Spangler states that "manifestation must not be seen as a way of getting what we need, but as an opportunity of being what we are in our true individuality, thus bringing the realization of that individuality closer and more concretely into our consciousness. Then you can think of a need not as a lack but something that permits you to be, and nourishes the wholeness within you to express as God. The only need we really have is for God to express Himself through us by means of what we create through the living of our lives. Our Beingness is the creative spirit of God, a potentiality waiting to become an actuality." Everything in our external world is created from our inner essence — our thoughts, ideas, emotions, and feelings. We can create good or bad, positive or negative experiences, based on the thoughts we entertain all day. We are forever creating, therefore every thought we think becomes a prayer, because it is materialized in our daily lives.

Another aspect of manifestation is the process of releasing potential; we manifest what already exists. The answer is potential within the problem. As health is the potential within illness; abundance is the potential within poverty. "Manifestation is a means of bringing the reality of potential into the reality of actuality, availability, and activity.

It is something we do all the time through our living. One important way we do this is through our speech. Language is a tool and vehicle of manifestation. It gives form through sounds, letters, shapes on paper to energies of the mind, feeling and the spirit. God manifested the earth through the power of Language. At the beginning of the Gospel of John, it reads: "In the beginning was the Word, and the Word was with God and the Word was God." Likewise, in Hebrews, 11:3, we read: "By faith we perceive that the universe was fashioned by the word of God, so that the visible came forth from the invisible. Likewise, we also manifest through our language, the language of speech, thought, feeling, expression, action and being. Speech is a creative tool. This is why spiritual teachers tell us to be aware of our language, of what we say and how we say it. We are manifestors. We are always manifesting when we talk, and the forms we make visible to others through our speech reveals a lot about our inner state. It determines the nature of the world we experience and attract to ourselves. This is the reason to keep our speech pure, clear, positive, sacred, and use it economically so as to conserve and magnify its power.

Which is why we should avoid purposeless negative talking. An abundance of speech using the wrong words may lead to a poverty of manifestation.

There is power in the words we speak. So, watch your thoughts, they are precursors of words you speak. Let your words be positive, and uplifting, state what you want to occur, not what you don't want to occur.

Gratitude is powerful. Gratitude is the sharing or expressing of joy for the good we have already received. We can give tangibles such as money, food, or clothing, or we can give intangibles such as kindness, under standing, love, forgiveness, consideration, generosity, peace, or harmony. What are you grateful for?

My Gratitude Page
In my notebook I will write daily at least one thing I am grateful for:

Love is powerful. When we love all people, there are no enemies out there to harm us. When we reach out to others in love, it is returned to us in the form of connections, positive relationships, support, and concern. Since God is Love, everything good and perfect begins to flow into our life. Remember to give of your good and it will return to you over flowing in abundance.

Always trust the small voice inside you. You can only be as successful as your mental patterns, as good as your intention, and as progressive as your ideas. It all start within you. The kingdom of God is within each of us. It will speak privately to each of us, about what is our mission in life, when we still our mind and allow ourselves to be a suitable vessel. Learn to trust your first thought, regardless of what others may say, for the spirit within you will tell you what to d.

Molefi Asante states, "there are two things over which you have complete dominion, authority, and control, it is your mind and your mouth."

Iyanla Vanzant in her book on daily meditations, *Acts Of Faith*, says "Your mind is an instrument. A precious gift to be valued and cared for. You are not always in control of what goes into your mind, but only you can determine what stays there. If you allow negativity to pervade in your mind, you will produce that negativity with your mouth. Your mouth is the mechanism that reveals how well you care for your mind." The conditions in your life stem from the most dominant thoughts of which you speak. Nothing has a hold on your mind that you cannot break free of. Since your mind responds to what is said to you, you can speak to the conditions in your life. When they are wanted, give thanks. When they are unwanted, demand they change; affirm, I am in control of my mind and mouth.

> *For no man can be blessed without the acceptance of his head.*
> —YORUBA PROVERB

To be in control of yourself is the beginning of wisdom. Self-control is control of one's emotions, one's desires and one's actions. Have you ever lost your temper? Have you ever said something and later regretted saying it? Have you ever acted in a way that later you were ashamed of? Most of us have if we are truthful. This happens when we try to protect our ego, save face, or prevent ourselves from appearing foolish.

Nobody is unhappier than a continual reactor. Because his center of emotional gravity is not rooted within himself, where it belongs, but in the world outside him. His emotional temperature is always being raised or lowered by the social environment around him and he is at the mercy of the climate.

Praise gives this person a feeling of euphoria, which is false, because it does not come from self-approval. Criticism depresses them because it confirms their secretly low opinion of themselves. Snubs hurt them, and any suspicion of unpopularity rouses them to anger or bitterness.

We cannot achieve serenity or inner peace until we become master of our actions, reactions and attitudes. If you let another person determine whether you will be gracious, or rude, elated, or depressed, you lose control over your personality, and your personality is all you possess.

Have you ever been afraid to admit you were wrong or afraid to tell someone you loved them? Have you ever avoided a task because it was difficult or uncomfortable? Have you ever been afraid to tell the truth to anyone or to yourself? It takes courage to look at the unpleasant and painful parts of ourselves. But look we must. Courage is our response to face and deal with anything we consider dangerous, difficult, or painful.

Words Of Wisdom

> *Sooner or later, people with any wisdom discover that life is a mixture of good days and bad, win and lose, victory and defeat, give and take.*
> —ANON

Walter Dill Scott of Northwestern University said, "Success or failure in any undertaking is caused more by the mental attitude — even more than by capacities."

> *Man Is What He Believes*
> —ANTON CHEKHOV

Understanding Ourselves, Each Other,
And The Divine Plan For Our Life

Write in your notebook saying what

1. My Current Realities Are:
2. Major Disappointments For Me in Life/Business Are:
3. My Present Hopes/Future Possibilities Are:

Prayer Treatment For Right Employment

There is a place for me in the job market and I expect to find it. It is the right place, the position for which I am both qualified and ready. Within me as I speak is an intelligence that knows what is my right job/employment, where it is, and when I will find it. I now call upon this power to guide me in the right direction. I release all anxiety. I await with confidence as I listen to the Divine intuition which will show me the next step to take. I accept my right employment now. I am open-minded and willing to be guided. —ANON

The key to getting what you desire in life is the principle of transmutation. Learn to **transmute the undesirable into the desirable**, through your **thoughts (desire)** ➜ **beliefs** ➜ **actions.** Remember, desire and determination will bring any goal within your reach.

Create A Spiritual Foundation To Handle Adversity
Thoughts are things and the law of mind action that thoughts produce after their kind is true. Our intentions are our thoughts looking for a goal.

Our mind changes our body chemistry so much, that we are unable to perform an activity, as normally done, even with a good night's sleep. However, we can renew ourselves by telling ourselves we are in danger, or having a desired or longed for opportunity. Our inner spirit renews and makes new everything about us.

There is Power in the spoken word: Every time you speak, you influence your world. You are either building your world or tearing it down by the thoughts you think hourly.

By your words you will be justified, and by your words you will be condemned. —MATTHEW 12:37

Regardless of what you do in life, you will experience some adverse conditions. That is because life is risky, and the human condition is beset with problems. If you want to live a life without problems, you should have never been born. The bible say man was born to trouble. The only people who don't have problems are dead people. God never promised us a rose garden, however he did say he would be with us through the end of time. Which means we are never alone regardless the problems we may encounter.

I know from my experiences, that I have not asked God's help with all of my problems, and I have tried to solve them by myself. The human intellect can not solve some problem. Some conditions we encounter are too complex to be solved by the human mind, and needs the spiritual dimension of a higher plane, which I refer to as Divine intervention. And Divine intervention always uses faith as a foundation to support our faltering ego and unstable intellect. It does this through our faith.

Faith is belief in a power greater than ourselves. It is believing in a higher power/force, when all objective data say there is no hope. It is your reliance on God to intercede on your behalf, when you have done all you can humanly do. You must know that things will work out, in spite of the circumstances due to your positive belief. The power of believing is powerful, however the bible says that faith without works is no good. Positive belief, faith must always be followed by action to be effective. Positive thinking has two components that make it work, faith and a positive expectancy of good.

When you do everything for the glory of God, your energy and skills will be at its highest level. 1 Corinthians 10:31, says "whatsoever ye do, do all to the glory of God, whatever your task is, put your whole heart into it, as into work done for the Lord."

Begin It Now

*Until one is committed, there is hesitancy, the chance to draw
  back, always ineffectiveness.*
*Concerning all acts of initiative, there is one elementary truth
  — the ignorance of which kills countless ideas and splendid
  plans:*
*That the moment one definitely commits oneself, then
  providence moves too. All sorts of things occur to help one
  that would never otherwise have occurred.*
*A whole stream of events issues from the decision, raising in
  one's favor all manner of unforeseen incidents and
  meetings and material assistance which no man could have
  dreamed would have come his way.*
*Whatever you can do, or dream you can, begin it. Boldness has
  genius, power and magic in it. Begin it now!*
                                        —GOETHE

We are more than a mere body with a brain, heart, nerves, bones,
and blood vessels. We are multi dimensional. We are body,
emotions, and spirit. The body is the vehicle that our soul
expresses through. The soul uses and need all parts of the body,
and our emotions to bring forth its Divine Essence. This is why we
feel frustrated when we hold back, or block the larger power's plan
for us, and Gods' presence to manifest in our lives. All of us were
created for greatness, because the indwelling power within us is
great. However, because of our limited, distorted, and
preoccupation with the small ego self, we fail to let the great
Divine Power within us burst forth. We are so mesmerized with
our smallness and sense of inadequacy, that we cannot set our egos
aside, to allow the Glory and Majesty of God to shine through us.

   This Divine Power will never force itself on us. It has to be
invited into our lives. And as long as we are in control of the
affairs of our life, it will let us be in control. It will not take away
our free will. Because we are Gods' ourselves, on a lower level.
We were created in the image and likeness of God. Therefore we

have all the attributes of God. So we have the power to create good, bad, or evil in our lives by the thoughts we hourly entertain. If the thoughts we dwell on are wholesome, uplifting, positive, optimist, spiritual, loving and divine; there is divine order and perfection, in our body, mind, and affairs. Which manifest as perfect health, happiness, success, prosperity, abundance, peace, harmony, high self-esteem and positive relationships.

Everything we have in our lives is a direct result of our past and present thoughts. We are the sum total of our conscious and subconscious thoughts; the cultural beliefs of our ancestors, the collective beliefs of society, and our inner Spiritual Self. Most of us are unaware of our spiritual dimension. So we rarely allow it to come forth until late in life, when we are in our sixties or seventies. Our Spiritual Self expresses through us as intuition, and inspiration. It is the small voice within that speaks to us and guides us to do what is just, right, and the highest good of all. It is never concerned with our intellect, ego, righteousness, or self-centeredness. The Divine Self concerns itself with what you need to do to be your Christ Self.

It may sometimes prompt you to apologize to someone, as I recently did, when my Higher Self revealed to me during my meditation, that I had wronged some one. I would have never noticed my error had I not invited my Divine Self to take control of my life; because my human self was causing me a lot of pain and hardship in my relationships. My old ways of relating to others were ineffective, and did not produce the results I wanted. Therefore, I was ready and willing to change. God exists at the center of our being, and remains dormant until we invite the Holy Spirit, to take control.

The first step to take, so your Divine Self comes through, is to control the kind of thoughts you think. Pay attention to the kind of thoughts you think moment by moment. Are they negative, self defeating, limited, selfish thoughts, or is your mind filled with thoughts of love for your fellow man, joy, health, peace, happiness, success, prosperity, abundance, harmony, high self-esteem and positive relationships.

Ask yourself: Am I allowing my greatness to come forth, or do I allow my thoughts to dwell on failure, lack, limitation, envy, jealousy, sickness, greed, or poverty? Am I paralyzed with fear that my needs will not be met? Do I think God is apart from me, and unconcerned about my welfare? Do I feel God loves me unconditionally, twenty-four hours a day, even when I do wrong or make a mistake.

Our subconscious mind is working at all times to bring forth the thoughts, images, and impressions we have given it. There are three things that have to change before an idea can be transformed into action. The idea, the feelings surrounding the idea and the action. If you want something very badly, and your mind considers it positively and confidently, you can bring life to it through your feelings. Then the life in your feelings unlocks the life in your idea to give it energy. This energy is what is called enthusiasm, and this enthusiasm directs and compels you into action. All ideas need the fuel of your feeling nature to be transformed into action. This is why Jesus stated "Faith without works is dead." Ideas are a dime a dozen, until you give them life through your feeling nature. When an idea (thought) is ignited by your feelings, it takes on life, and anything that is alive will be sustained. So hold onto your dreams to make them come alive.

Hold On To That Dream

Hold to that dream, don't ever let it go...
For it is your strength and courage when traveling
  down life's road.
Patience is a virtue, but hope is far better,
So hold onto that dream, no matter how old.
      —MIRIAM MEDINA, OLD BRIDGE, NJ

Success is not for the faint of heart. To be successful at anything in life, it will require determination, commitment, and a willingness to do whatever it takes to reach your goal. Otherwise you will have limited success, or no success. An example of this was my goal to be a highly paid, motivational speaker. I love speaking, but I equally loved being at home, and I did not like to travel. My speaking career was stifled, because I did not like staying in hotels, and eating restaurant food. It took me almost seven years before I was willing to travel out of town to speak. Your success will be hampered by your unwillingness to do all the things required of you to be top notch in your chosen endeavor. Why don't you sit down now, and *make a list in your notebook* of all the things you may have to do to accomplish your goal/s. Circle all the things you are willing to do, and put a square or box around the things you would rather not do or want someone else to do.

Internal-Comfort Zones

A comfort zone is an internal regulation that alerts you to either feeling "out of place" or comfortable with a situation.

When you feel out of place, it shuts off your recall, and the harder you try, the less you remember.

The first thing to go is your voice.

Comfort zones are like thermostats, so listen to the words and assimilate; more importantly listen to your tone of voice.

Meaningful and lasting change will only take place if it comes from within; start with your self-image (inside), the change will then take place (outside).

As we imprint the new, we become dissatisfied with the old.

On Adversity

Things my mother said to me:

"Where there is a will there is a way."

"Praise God in all things." Say Thank you God when problems and adverse conditions come you way.

"When people are mean to you, feed them with kindness, love, and understanding."

Things I Have Learned About Life and Living

"You are somebody in God's presence. There is no place you can go where you are not in the presence of God."

What we think and feel we create. Our thoughts are powerful.

"Surrender your will, to hear the still voice within you."

"Anticipation, tension, anxiety, worry, or a need for certainty, all are a form of fear. They are founded on a lack of Faith in God."

Most human sickness seems connected to some mistake, or error in one's lifestyle.

You cannot compare the success of another person to your success. So know who you are and what is important to you. Then decide what you want, and why you want it. Ask yourself why is it important to you to accomplish the goal you desire. To be fully alive, you must always have a goal or something you want to achieve. Our dreams, give us hope, passion, a future, yearning, drive, anticipation, enthusiasm (our fire) and energy (healthy tension). Then you couple these with faith (unwavering belief that what you desire will happen) and you have greatness. Constantly seek to make life better for yourself and your fellowman. I like the way Charles Conn states it, "We must never be ashamed of wanting more. We must never be embarrassed by our hunger. We must never believe that to strive for a better world, or a better life, is somehow an act of disloyalty to the old one. We must always be willing to be hungry — hungry to sing a better song, write a better letter, bowl a higher score, make a bigger profit, set a better example, give more support to the causes, organizations, and people we believe in."

The Impossible Dream

To dream the impossible dream,
To fight the unbeatable foe,
To bear with unbearable sorrow,
To run where the brave dare not go,

To right the unrightable wrong,
To love pure and chaste from afar,
To try when your arms are too weary,
To reach the unreachable star.

This is my quest, to follow that star,
No matter how hopeless, no matter how far,
To fight for the right without question or pause,
To be willing to march into hell for a heavenly cause,
And I know I'll only be true to this glorious quest,
That my heart will lie peaceful and calm when
    I'm laid to my rest,

And the world will be better for this
That one person scorned and covered with scars,
Still strove with their last ounce of courage,
To reach the unreachable star.

Take A Chance

Even a turtle gets nowhere until he sticks his neck out.
On the plains of hesitation, bleach the bones of
*   unnumbered thousands, who at the dawn of victory, sat*
*   down to wait and waiting died.*

Success is for those energetic enough to work for it.
Hopeful enough to look for it,
Patient enough to wait for it,
Brave enough to seize it,
And strong enough to hold it.   —ANON

Sooner or later we must realize there is no station, no one
place to arrive at once and for all. The true joy of life is the
trip. The station is only a dream. It constantly outdistances
us. "Relish the moment" is a good motto, especially when
coupled with Psalm 118-24: "This is the day which the
Lord hath made; we will rejoice and be glad in it*." It isn't*
the burdens of today that drive men mad. It is the regrets
over yesterday and the fear of tomorrow. Regret and fear
are twin thieves who rob us of today. So, stop pacing the
aisles and counting the miles. Instead, climb more
mountains, eat more ice cream, go barefoot more often,
swim more rivers, watch more sunsets, laugh more, cry
less. Life must be lived as we go along. The station will
come soon enough.
                —ROBERT J. HASTINGS

Are you ready for your greatness to come forth? Do you see
yourself as a winner or a loser? We need more winners. To be a
success in business you must live and breathe these words
"You must act as if it is impossible to fail."
                —ASHANTI PROVERB

Seven things that will destroy us: *Politics without principle; wealth without work; business without morality; pleasure without conscience; science without humanity; knowledge without character; and worship without sacrifice.*
—MOHANDAS K. GHANDI

Never downgrade yourself or your importance in life, and never allow others to berate you or make fun of you. You produce results in the world through your thoughts (desire), your feelings (passion), and your attitude (intention). Whatever you really want, or really don't want you will get. Your passion or fear gives you both.

Remember, God helps those who help themselves. To be a success in the business world, you will need high ambition, right thinking, positive and energetic action, individual initiative, patience, and a purpose for living. We were created to serve and be of service to our fellow man. When Napoleon Hill pressed Andrew Carnegie for the single key to achievement, he stated "the greatest service that one can render to God is by helping others." If you help enough people get what they want in life, they will guarantee your success in business.

Bibliography

Brown Lillian. *Your Public Best*. Newmarket Press, New York, 18 East 48th Street, New York, N.Y. 10017

Conn Charles Paul. *Making It Happen*. Fleming H. Revell Company, Old Tappan, New Jersey.

Holmes Ernest. This Thing Called Life. Dodd, Mead, & Company, 79 Madison Avenue, New York, N. Y. 10016

"Prosperity Connection," FER Publications, P.O. Box 1023, Palos Verdes CA 90274

Spangler David, The Laws of Manifestation, Findhorn Publications, Morayshire, Scotland

Testimonials

The information in the book helped me to Say Hello to my Greatness. —DEE SANFORD, SPEAKER, AND TELEVISION PERSONALITY

The information in the book was inspiring and insightful —TOYA HICKS

The information helped me to Say Goodbye to my Smallness. —BOBBY CARNEY

www.ingramcontent.com/pod-product-compliance
Lightning Source LLC
Chambersburg PA
CBHW031950190326
41519CB00007B/745